GLASS CANOPIES

TUTE of Art & Design

2004

11 MAY 2006   27 APR 2006

GLASS CANOPIES

MARITZ VANDENBERG

DETAIL IN BUILDING

A.D. ACADEMY EDITIONS

DETAIL IN BUILDING
Advisory Panel: Maritz Vandenberg, Christopher Dean, Christopher McCarthy
Series Editor: Michael Spens

ACKNOWLEDGEMENTS
The following people gave me invaluable assistance. For this I thank them, though all mistakes are of course my own.
Tony Hunt, Alan Jones and Chris Herring of Anthony Hunt Associates; David Button; James Woodrough of Davis Langdon and Everest; Tim Macfarlane, Philip Wilson and Priscilla Trench of Dewhurst Macfarlane & Partners; Frank Hensky of Emmer Pfenniger Partner AG; Peter Knight of Eurostar (UK) Limited; Michael Jones, Katy Harris and Marta Badia-Marin of Sir Norman Foster and Partners; Dieter Früh of Früh Metallbau; Andrew Whalley, Diane Hutchinson and Brian Parkes of Nicholas Grimshaw & Partners; Bill Dunster and Clare Stevens of Sir Michael Hopkins and Partners; Pauline Shirley, Annette O'Brien and Paul Simpson of the Ove Arup Partnership; John Colvin of Pilkington UK Limited; Armin Waberseck and Patrick Lalor of Mero Raumstruktur; Ian Ritchie and Simon Conolly of Ian Ritchie Architects; Darryl Mountford and Katja Stadler of Seele GmbH; Peter Muncaster of Taylor Woodrow Construction Southern Limited; and Hiroshi Okamoto of Ushida Findlay Partnership.
I am particularly grateful to Dennis Gilbert for permission to use his photographs of the University of Cambridge Faculty of Law and Bracken House, and to Nikkei Architecture and Kobayashi Photography Studio for permission to use their photographs of Tokyo Forum.
Finally I wish to record my special thanks to Michael Spens (who commissioned this book) and to his colleagues Maggie Toy and Ramona Khambatta (for her skilful editing) and Mario Bettella and Gualtiero Gualtieri (for an excellent design).

All technical diagrams were drawn by the author. Photographs are reproduced by permission of: p2 Royal Botanic Gardens and Andrew McRobb; pp8-9 Ove Arup Partnership; p12 Ove Arup Partnership and Kurt Gahler; pp13 (above), 16, 19, 50, 54 Denis Gilbert; cover, pp13 (below), 14, 36, 45, 47, 49 Mero Raumstruktur; pp22, 34 Eurostar (UK) Limited; pp32, 33 Anthony Hunt Associates; pp42-44, 46, 48 Seele GmbH; pp56, 59 (below left), 61 Nikkei Architecture and Kobayashi Photography Studio; p59 (above and below right) Dewhurst Macfarlane & Partners.

Cover: Von Gerkan, Marg & Partners and Ian Ritchie Architects, Central Entrance Hall, Exhibition and Conference Centre, Leipzig
Page 2: Richard Turner, Palm House, Kew, Surrey

First published in Great Britain in 1997 by
ACADEMY EDITIONS
a division of John Wiley & Sons,
Baffins Lane, Chichester,
West Sussex PO19 1UD

Other Wiley Editorial Offices
New York • Weinheim • Brisbane • Singapore • Toronto

Distributed to the trade in the United States of America by
NATIONAL BOOK NETWORK, INC
4720 Boston Way, Lanham, Maryland 20706

ISBN 0-471-97688-1

Printed and bound in Singapore

CONTENTS

BRIEF HISTORY

The history of the glass roof goes back to roughly the end of the eighteenth century, when a five-thousand-year-old material began to be used in architecturally unprecedented ways. This development was centred in an evolving new building type – the glass-framed horticultural conservatory.

The idea of the greenhouse was not new but especially after about 1815 (when industrially-produced iron framing became available) private orangeries and winter gardens became popular features on the country estates and urban gardens of the wealthy, especially in Britain. Within a few decades early small-scale prototypes evolved into glasshouses capable of housing large exotic plants such as palms, and by the late nineteenth century most leading European cities could boast cathedral-sized planthouses in their public parks and botanical gardens, clad and roofed almost entirely in glass.

There was a particular spurt of development after 1845 when England abolished excise duty on glass. One of the first buildings to take advantage of cheaper glass was Richard Turner's Palm House at Kew (1845-48) and this shapely, delicately ribbed structure achieved an elegance of design that has seldom been surpassed to this day [page 2].

The second major structure in England to take advantage of cheaper glass was Richard Turner and Joseph Locke's Lime Street station in Liverpool (1849-50), which transpired to be the birth of a second wholly new building type. There was no architectural precedent for the railway terminus and the model that evolved took the form of a head building, designed as a palazzo or some other borrowing from traditional architecture, backed by a functional iron-and-glass shed that stood completely outside the traditional canon, as new in its way (although usually more opaque and less glassy) as the horticultural glasshouse. London,

the world's first rail-based metropolis, produced two of the finest early train sheds – Isambard Kingdom Brunel's Paddington of 1854 and WH Barlow and RM Ordish's 75-metre wide St Pancras of 1868, then the largest-spanning structure in history.

A third type of glass roof to develop in the nineteenth century was the street arcade. The first example actually appeared at the surprisingly early date of 1799 in the Passage du Caire, Paris. The French had seen covered streets during their conquest of Egypt the previous year and promptly applied the idea of the 'outside interior' in a Paris shopping street, a crude and primitive design (it still exists) but the forerunner of glass-roofed arcades and galleria such as Fontaine's Galérie d'Orleans in Paris (1829), the Galleria in Milan (1865-67) and subsequent examples in Berlin (1871-73), Naples (1887-89) and throughout the world.

Finally there was the exhibition hall, most spectacularly represented by Paxton's Crystal Palace (1851) and the Paris International Exhibitions of 1855, 67 and 89. The latter was the climax, containing the famous Halle des Machines with its 115-metre span, huge three-pinned iron arches and a translucent glass roof.

All these building types were utilitarian in nature, 'engineering' rather than 'architecture', and the acceptance of the glass roof into polite architecture came but slowly. An early small example was the delightful little glass-domed portico on the street facade of John Claudius Loudon's house at 3-5 Porchester Terrace in London (1823-24, still extant); while the first really large glass roof in an architecturally acceptable context was that of the Bon Marche store in Paris (1876, since destroyed in a fire).

The above developments may be traced more fully in the references listed on page 64, while we pass to the practicalities of present day design. We look first at functional requirements, then at aesthetic factors.

FUNCTIONAL REQUIREMENTS

OVERALL REQUIREMENTS

A glass roof or canopy must satisfy many functional requirements – too many to discuss adequately in this short book. The headings below form a useful checklist and each of the concepts listed is clearly explained in David Button and Brian Pye's authoritative *Glass in Building*. The book also has chapters on structural glass systems (dealing mainly with walls rather than roofs and canopies); glass and the environment; and glass terms, products and processes.

Once basic principles are understood, reference data for particular products will be found in the literature of leading manufacturers.

Visual functions:	admission of daylight
	view in and view out
	appearance
Thermal functions:	heat loss
	heat gain
	thermal balance
Mechanical functions:	durability of glass
	strength of glass
	wind and snow loads
	thermal stress
	human impact
	explosive loading
	bullet impact
	burglar attack
Other functions:	fire resistance
	sound insulation

AESTHETICS (handwritten annotation)

SAFETY REQUIREMENTS

The one functional requirement that must be discussed here is safety, a major issue in overhead glazing (the latter term used throughout this text to mean a single pane of glazing, or the lower pane of an insulating unit, in sloping or horizontal roofing applications in non-agricultural buildings).

Two factors are involved: (a) choice and specification of glazing and (b) the design of the support system.

TYPES OF GLAZING

Table 1 lists the main glass types from the strongest (1) to the weakest (4).

Glass Types	Description	Is it classified as a 'safety glass'?
1 Toughened glass (known in the USA as 'tempered glass').	A heat-treated glass that is four to five times as strong as float or patterned glass. Has the advantage of breaking into relatively safe dice rather than danger-ous shards when fractured; but the disadvantage that it cannot be cut, worked or drilled after toughening and must be ordered to precise dimensions.	Yes
2 Heat strengthened glass.	Twice or three times as strong as float or patterned glass; breaks into sharp-edge shards when fractured.	No
3 Float glass and patterned glass (the latter previously known as cast glass).	The two most commonly used types of annealed glass. Not particularly strong, and break into sharp shards when fractured.	No
4 Wired glass.	The weakest glass of all but has the advantage of holding together after fracture.	Yes
Any combination of the above glasses laminated to an interlayer of plastic such as polyvinyl butyral (pvb) will form a safety glass.		

Table 1 Characteristics of the main glass types

With regard to plastics, the principal types for architectural use are polycarbonate and polymethylmethacrylate or pmma (the latter more popularly known as acrylic, perspex or plexiglass).

These products have much the same degree of transparency as glass but in a structural sense are almost its opposite: whereas glass is very strong and very fragile, plastic is less strong but tougher. On the positive side, plastics are also lighter than glass (about 50 per cent the density), more easily formed, more easily handled, and have lower thermal conductivity. On the negative side they not only have less initial strength than glass but are further weakened by heat, including sunlight; are softer and are more subject to surface abrasion.

The most familiar use of polycarbonates on their own is in vandal-resistant rooflights and bus shelters but their characteristics can also be exploited in works of architectural distinction. The 1985 IBM Travelling Pavilion by Renzo Piano Work-shop with Ove Arup and Partners, a transparent vault formed of 34 polycarbonate pyramids, is a notably beautiful example [figures 1, 2a, 2b].

However, the best use of plastics tends to be not on their own but in combina-tion with glass, the strengths of each complementing the weaknesses of the other. There are two main types of glass/plastic composites:
• Laminated glass, consisting usually of two layers of glass laminated to an interlayer

1. 1985 IBM Travelling Pavilion

of plastic such as polyvinyl butyral (pvb), which offers substantially greater structural safety than any glass on its own.

• Sealed composite units which offer better U-values than all-glass constructions – see manufacturers' literature for details of specific products.

There may be exciting developments to come in the field of plastics and glass/plastic composites, see Michael Wigginton's *Glass in Architecture*.

CHOICE OF GLAZING

Appropriate glass types for particular situations are summarised in Table 2, based on information kindly supplied by Pilkington UK Limited.

Situation	Glass type
1 Roofs for agricultural greenhouses.	3mm thick annealed horticultural glass.
2 Glazing at heights of up to 5m above floor level in single storey buildings. Includes conservatories.	If single glazing: (a) toughened* (b) laminated or (c) wired glass. If multi-layer insulating units: Lower pane – as for single glazing. Upper pane – if the lower pane is toughened glass then the upper pane should be toughened, laminated or wired glass. If the lower pane is laminated or wired glass then the upper pane may be any glass type.
3 Glazing at heights of 5-13m above floor level. Includes medium-height atria and larger conservatories	If single glazing: (a) laminated or wired glass or (b) non-laminated toughened* glass provided that panes are not more than 3sqm in area or 6mm thick, in which case the glass should be laminated. If multi-layered insulating units: Lower pane – as for single glazing. Upper pane – if the lower pane is laminated or wired glass then the upper pane may be any glass type. If the lower pane is toughened glass then the upper pane should be (a) laminated or wired glass or (b) non-laminated toughened glass provided that panes are not more than 3sqm in area or 6mm thick, in which case the glass should be laminated.
4 Glazing at heights more than 13m above floor level.	If single glazing: (a) laminated or (b) wired glass If multi-layer insulating units: Lower pane – as for single glazing; upper pane – any glass type.

* If toughened glass is used as overhead single glazing or the lower pane of insulating units, it is recommended that heat-soaking be specified. Toughened glass should never be used either as overhead single glazing or the lower pane of insulating units in situations over swimming pools because fragments of broken glass can cause major damage to pumps and equipment.

Table 2 Appropriate glass types for various overhead situations

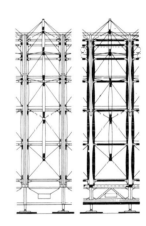

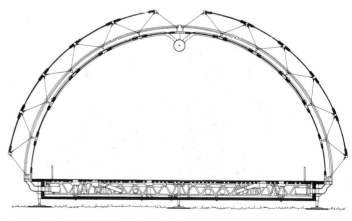

2a and 2b. 1985 IBM Travelling Pavilion

It will be seen that, except in low buildings like agricultural greenhouses, overhead glazing must always consist of a safety glass. The latter are of two types – glasses that disintegrate into harmless 'dice' after fracture (toughened glass), and

glasses that hold together after fracture (laminated glass and wired glass).

Toughened glass has an excellent safety record and may be specified with confidence, but must be laminated if used in large panes at a great height.

Laminated glass of any kind is safer than a single sheet of toughened glass, and the highest degree of safety will be delivered by laminated toughened glass.

Wired glass is safe for all overhead use, particularly in fire-risk situations.

TYPES OF SUPPORT SYSTEM

The main types of support systems are the following:

• Framed systems, in which the glass pane rests in a surrounding frame.

• Bolt and plate systems, in which toughened glass panes are held by bolts and small metal patch plates at their corners and pane-to-pane joints are sealed with silicone. See, for instance, the Bracken House entrance canopy on pages 50-55. Except in small structures it must be ensured that the glass plane is isolated from movements in the support system.

• Planar systems (a registered name of Pilkington UK), in which frameless toughened glass panes are held only by countersunk bolt fixings which are designed to absorb and protect the glass from movement in the underlying structure. The flush glass surface offers good cleanability as well as a pleasingly sheer appearance.

• Stuck-back systems, in which the glass is bonded to a frame using structural silicone sealant – see, for instance, the Cambridge Faculty of Law on pages 16-21. Factory-assembly is recommended to ensure bond quality.

DESIGN OF SUPPORT SYSTEM

If a tailor-made solution is required, architects should turn to experienced consultants [see the Appendix on page 15] for design guidance. However, for simple situations the following five generalisations apply:

Allowance for Movement

Because glass is brittle and unable to redistribute load like metals and plastics, it cannot accommodate local overstressing and all movement in the supporting frame must be absorbed by flexible joints. In small canopies such as at Bracken House [pages 50-55] and the Tokyo Forum [pages 56-63]) compressible pane-to-pane joints may suffice, but in large roofs such as Waterloo International Rail Terminal [pages 22-35] or Leipzig Entrance Hall [pages 36-49] highly sophisticated sliding or pivoting fixings may be required to prevent movements in the steel frame being transferred into the glass and breaking the latter.

Stability of Structural Backgrounds

Arising from the above point, almost the most important single thing the designer can do to avoid later detailing headaches is provide a stable building frame for the envisaged glass claddings. Sometimes this is impossible – as at Waterloo, for the reasons explained on pages 22-35. Yet it is worth remembering that the springier the supporting structure, the more complex and expensive the glazing fixings.

Clearance around Pane Edges

If panes are held in a surrounding framework there should be enough clearance around the glass to accommodate tolerances and thermal movement. Rules of thumb suggest at least 3 millimetres for single glazing and 5 millimetres for double-glazed units, the dimensions increasing with the size of pane. The glass edges should rest on a bearing surface at least equal to the glass thickness and never less than 6 millimetres for single glazing or 12 millimetres for double-glazed units.

Adequate Size for Clip Fixings

If panes are held in clip fixings, each clip should cover a sufficient area and be suitably positioned to avoid any risk of local overstressing of the glass.

Metal Bolts Passing through Glass

If panes are held by metal plates plus a bolt that passes through the glass, the hole will be a weak point and toughened glass (drilled before toughening) must be used. The metal plates must be separated from the glass by non-compressible gaskets and a nylon or similar bush should be inserted between bolt and glass to prevent the metal bolt from contacting the edges of the hole.

Glass-to-Metal Contact

In all situations, glass-to-metal contact is inadvisable and there should be a softer interface between the two.

COST

At 1997 prices, excluding professional fees and VAT, erected costs/sqm on plan for a flat or faceted glass roof were approximately as follows. Single glazed roof, including aluminium framework but excluding support steel (for which add £100-£120) £250-£400; double glazed roof £350-£500; double glazed planar roof (including the structural frame) £700-£900. On the same basis, costs for single glazed canopies over entrances or walkways ranged from £500-£700, to £1,000 or £2,000 for small canopies with a high architectural content. These figures are reproduced by permission of Davis Langdon and Everest, London.

AESTHETIC CONSIDERATIONS

THE ISSUE OF TRANSPARENCY

As a large book could be written on the aesthetics of design, we will concentrate on a single issue that dominates architects' concerns in relation to glass: transparency. The questions to be asked include: how much transparency? transparency from which viewing angles and under what conditions? what kind of transparency? and transparency how modified? One way of discussing the issue is to sketch a spectrum of possibilities: at one end the glass membrane that is practically invisible ('not there'); at the other the membrane that powerfully asserts its presence; and between these outer poles many intermediate permutations.

THE GLASS PLANE THAT IS 'NOT THERE'

A central dream of modernism has been to exploit fully the transparency of glass – to use it as a sheet of 'frozen air' that keeps the rain out and the warmth in while remaining invisible. Virtually invisible canopies are possible provided they are small enough to be held at the edges only with no need for visible intermediate supports, but even then severely practical problems arise:

• The glass or plastic will be invisible only while free of dirt or dust; and only while the surface is unmarked by scratches. With plastics, even the process of cleaning may gradually abrade the surface and destroy its theoretical invisibility.

• Complete invisibility depends on the light coming predominantly from the opposite side to that of the viewer. If light falls mostly from the viewer's side of the glass, or if a bright sky casts veiling reflections on the viewer's side, then the surface immediately becomes visible. Anti-reflectant coatings, which can reduce reflections at normal incidence to perhaps one-eighth the usual figure, will reduce but may not eliminate this problem.

THE GLASS PLANE THAT IS 'HALF THERE'

One intermediate possibility is the glass membrane treated as an almost invisible sheet, identified only by points within its surface, with a support system hovering a few centimetres away. The following then become key issues:

• How *much* of a support system? If a pronounced feeling of lightness and trans-

1. View of the Chur bus and railway station, Switzerland, 1992. Architects: Richard Brosi and Robert Obrist

2. Detail of the canopy at Chur

parency is wanted, Ian Ritchie Architects suggest that the structural silhouette should cover no more than 15 per cent of the field of view when looking perpendicularly through the glazing. See in this connection the Chur bus and railway station [figures 1,2] and Leipzig Entrance Hall on pages 36-49, both of which were designed to this criterion.

• What *kind* of structural support system? Particularly with large structures it is easy for the support system to become such a confused cat's cradle of structural members that the clean transparency originally aimed for is destroyed. In their excellent book *Structural Glass*, Peter Rice and Hugh Dutton recommend that the overall system be rigorously divided into a hierarchy of separate 'layers' based on structural logic. Thus, there could be a primary framework of large-diameter members carrying heavy loads over a long span; then, visually separated from that, a secondary framework of slender members supporting small well-defined segments of the canopy; and finally, again as a separate layer, the glass shell with its support points. The Leipzig and Chur roofs illustrate such an approach.

• The *location* of the support system. This must be outside the plane of the glass to achieve the desired effect, but on which side – the upper (as at Leipzig) or the lower (as at Chur)? The decision may be influenced by functional considerations such as structural behaviour or ease of assembly but the designer should also consider on which side of the structure most onlookers will be, from which side most light will fall, and exactly what he wishes the effect to be.

A second intermediate possibility is the glass shell with glass blade supports, seen for instance in the Tokyo Forum canopy on pages 56-63 and in several frontier-pushing projects by the architect Rick Mather and the engineers Dewhurst Macfarlane & Partners [eg figure 3]. Idealists may yearn for such all-glass structures to be made near-invisible by the application of advanced design skills but in practice glass edges and interpane joints will show and the many differently orientated glass surfaces will inevitably pick up reflections.

3. Keats Grove, London

THE GLASS PLANE THAT ASSERTS ITS PRESENCE

Here we reach the other end of the spectrum where, instead of pretending not to be there, the glass membrane asserts and makes a positive virtue of its presence. It can do so in four ways:

• By combining with a framing system – a relatively unassertive example being the Community Centre at Bad Neustadt [figures 4, 5]. The framing system can either be in the same plane as the glass, in which case viewers from both sides will see a cellular structure with a definite surface texture created by the raised ribs [page 2]; or on the inside of the glass plane, in which case viewers on the outside will see (during the daytime) a smooth glassy carapace [figure 4].

• By drawing attention to its surface. The glass surface can be given a positive

4. Community Centre, Bad Neustadt

architectural character by surface texturing – acid etching or sandblasting – or by screen printing, all of which make the glass luminous instead of transparent. Alternatively, it can be given a mirror finish, making the glass reflective. In future there may be more exciting surface treatments such as dichroic coatings, holographic films and electrochromic or other switchable transmission films. These possibilities are discussed in Michael Wigginton's *Glass in Architecture*.

• By drawing attention to its substance. Examples include body-coloured or opaque glass, glass made of fused recycled granules, wired glass, etc.

• By geometry. Although completely transparent, the pyramidal polycarbonate panes in the 1986 IBM Travelling Pavilion [page 8] are made visible by faceted reflections and these combine with the elegant overall design (slender warm-coloured beech arches with cast aluminium nodes and stainless steel fixings) to create a crystalline effect that is extremely appealing.

Any of the above approaches can be combined, witness the gothic window (not a roof or canopy but the principle applies) in which richly coloured fragments of glass are embedded in a strong framework of black leading. While letting through light and effectively exploiting the magical qualities of glass, here is a glass membrane that powerfully asserts its presence and makes no attempt to disappear.

A DREAM OF THE FUTURE

Perhaps, if enough architects foreswear the banal and thoughtless use of a miraculous material we see all around, ponder the issues touched on above, and above all study the work of the best designers, we may still in part realise the dreams of the German visionary Paul Scheerbart (1863-1915) who yearned to 'remove the enclosed quality of the spaces within which we live. This can be done only through the introduction of a glass architecture that lets the sunlight and the light of the moon and stars into our rooms not merely through a few windows but simultaneously through the greatest possible number of walls that are made entirely of glass – coloured glass'.

Imagining the beauty of the earth if glass architecture were everywhere, he wrote: 'It would be as though the earth clad itself in jewelry of brilliants and enamel. The splendour is absolutely unimaginable. And we should then have on earth more exquisite things than the gardens of the Arabian Nights. Then we should have a paradise on earth and would not need to gaze longingly at the paradise in the sky.'

We do not now think it sensible for all architecture to be constructed of glass but some of it should be, and for such cases Scheerbart's words still have the power to thrill and inspire.

5. Community Centre, Bad Neustadt

APPENDIX: SPECIALIST CONSULTANCIES

Specialist knowledge is required for the design of glass structures. Top talent is most easily identified by looking at the best current work and seeing who was responsible but the following short list of consultancies may help those in doubt. The list is in alphabetical order and does not pretend to be comprehensive.

United Kingdom

1   Anthony Hunt Associates, Gloucester House, 60 Dyer Street, Cirencester GL7 2PF. Tel: 00-44-1-285-655-858, fax: 00-44-1-285-650-479. General structural consultants, not glass specialists, but unusually experienced in leading-edge projects.

2   Brookes Stacey Randall Fursdon, 34 Bruton Place, London WIX 7AA. Tel 00-44-171-495-2081, Fax: 00-44-171-499-0733. Special expertise in the design of castings.

3   Dewhurst Macfarlane and Partners, 41 North Road, London N7 9DP. Tel: 00-44-171-609-9541, fax: 00-44-171-607-6419.

4   Ian Ritchie Architects, O Metropolitan Wharf, Wapping Wall, London E1 9SS. Tel: 00-44-171-481-4427, fax: 00-44-171-481-8200.

5   Ove Arup Partnership, 13 Fitzroy Street, London WIP 6BQ. Tel: 00-44-171-636-1531, fax: 00-44-171-580-3924.

Ireland

Sean Billings Associates, Fernside Mews, Killiney Hill Road, County Dublin, Eire. Tel: 00-353-1-285-7209, fax: 00-353-1-285-7044.

USA

James Carpenter Design Associates Inc, 145 Hudson Street, New York, NY 10013. Tel: 00-1-212-431-4318, fax: 00-1-212-431-4425.

Germany

Prof A Schlaich, Institut fur Konstruktion und Entwurf, Stuttgart University, Pfaffenwaldring 7, D70569, Stuttgart, Tel: 00-49-711-685-6227, fax: 0049-711-685-6968.

France

RFR (Rice Francis Ritchie), 4-6 Rue d'Enghien, 75010, Paris. Tel: 00-331-5-324-9100, fax: 00-331-5-324-1313.

The Netherlands

Prof Mick Eekhout, Octatube Space Structures BV, Rotterdamseweg 200, 2628 AS, Delft, The Netherlands. Tel: 00-15-256-9362, fax: 00-15-262-2300.

Fig 1

SIR NORMAN FOSTER & PARTNERS AND YRM ANTHONY HUNT ASSOCIATES

FACULTY OF LAW, UNIVERSITY OF CAMBRIDGE

Cambridge

In May 1990 the Faculty of Law and Institute of Criminology at the University of Cambridge held a limited architectural competition for two new buildings. A large floor area had to be fitted into a relatively small site area and the client required this to be done in a way that respected the setting, not intruding unduly into the established scene and skyline. The building was required to be highly energy-efficient.

Sir Norman Foster and Partners won the competition and proposed a Faculty of Law pavilion with a gross floor area of 9,000sqm accommodated in four storeys above and two storeys below ground level. A description of the building as a whole was published in the *Architectural Review* of March 1996 (pages 34-40) but we deal here only with the north facade.

Design Concept

The north facade is a cylindrical glazed shell that develops into a stainless steel roof just before it reaches its apex. The outer surface is glacially smooth [figure 4] and all structural members are located on the inside, forming a cool white lattice [figure 5]. The facade structure is a triangulated steel double Vierendeel truss spanning nearly 40 metres. 42 steelwork modules weighing two to four tons each were factory-made from straight 139.7 millimetre diameter tubes, and then erected on site. The outer booms (which bear the principal loads) are spaced at 3.9 metre centres; the inner ones (with the less demanding task of giving depth to the structural section) at 7.8 metres.

The sequence of elements forming the facade is as follows, starting from the outside:

• The outer skin consists of sealed double-glazed units [marked A on figure 9], triangular in shape and factory-bonded to similarly triangular aluminium frames B.

• Each of these pre-assembled triangular units is set into a structural aluminium carrier frame C, already in position on the building facade, as an on-site operation.

• The triangular carrier frames C are bolted to the tubular steel structure via a machined steel block at each of the lattice intersections, thus forming a series of six-way nodes which allow for simultaneous adjustment and tolerance in all three axes (ie, in six directions).

• After on-site assembly, the joints between the double-glazing units are given a final seal of silicone pointing protected by vulcanised silicone cover strips [figure 9].

Allowance for Structural Movement

The facade structure is fixed along the line

1. Faculty of Law, Cambridge

17

marked on figure 2 and is free to expand or contract from this line in response to thermal change. With a temperature differential of $\pm$ 25K, thermal movement is catered for thus:

In cold weather:

• Facade contraction due to low temperatures is absorbed by sliding joints in the carrier frames C. These spaces, 2 millimetres wide at the design temperature of 20°C, will expand to 6.6 millimetres with a temperature difference of -25k.

In hot weather:

• Initial expansion is absorbed by the joint space, which reduces from 2 millimetres at 20°C, to nil with a temperature difference of +11k.

• Then at temperature differences of +11K to +25K, with the joints closed up, the whole system will move with the length difference taken up at the facade ends.

The following design features allow for these movements and provide assembly tolerances:

• In the steel structure, each machined block D slides on steel pins which are fixed back to the tubular steel structure through slotted holes [figure 6], thus allowing two-way movement within the plane of the facade. Height adjustment perpendicular to the plane of the facade is achieved by turning the threaded insert as shown by arrows X on figure 9, allowing movement of up to 4 millimetres.

• The aluminium frames B and carrier frames C can move relative to each other as shown by the arrows Y (plus/minus 3mm) and Z (plus/minus 13 millimetres).

Cleaning and Maintenance

In addition to giving a smooth appearance, the joint detail shown in figure 9, with the outer glass leaf projecting beyond the inner, reduces dirt retention and maintenance requirements.

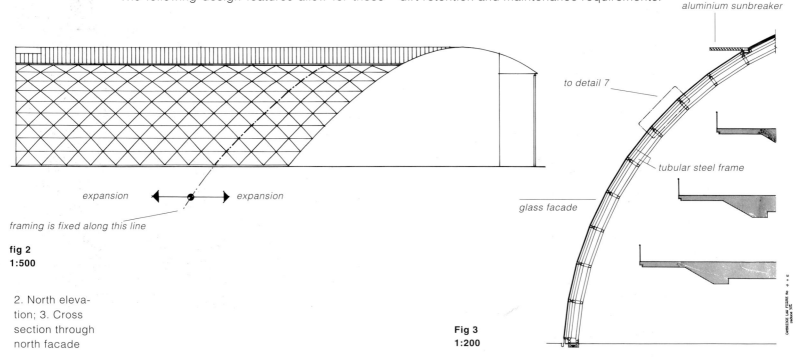

expansion ◄ ● ► *expansion*

framing is fixed along this line

fig 2
1:500

2. North elevation; 3. Cross section through north facade

aluminium sunbreaker

to detail 7

tubular steel frame

glass facade

Fig 3
1:200

SUMMARY DATA

Client:

University of Cambridge Estates Management

Timetable:

Competition: summer 1990; construction commenced summer 1993; construction completed autumn 1995

Architects:

Sir Norman Foster & Partners, London

Structural design:

YRM Anthony Hunt Associates, Cirencester

Cladding consultant:

Emmer Pfenniger Partner AG, Münchenstein, Switzerland

Quantity Surveyor:

Davis Langdon and Everest, London

Main contractor:

Taylor Woodrow Construction Southern Ltd

Cladding contractor:

Metallbau Früh (UK) Ltd, Carshalton

Steelwork fabricator:

Westbury Tubular Structures Ltd, Wetherby

Glass supplier:

Eckelt Glas, Linz

Specification of glass:

Glazing units comprise an outer pane of 10mm toughened glass, an inert gas space of 14mm, and an inner pane of 12.78mm laminated glass. In the lower seven rows of glazing the inner pane is low E coated; in the two top rows the inner pane is solar protected with a neutral metal coating

Glazing performance:

Light transmission: 63% to 72%; light reflection: 11%; total energy conduction (annual average): g=17%; shading coefficient (annual average): b=20%; heat transfer coefficient: $k=15W/m^2K$

Life expectancy:

Cladding 60 years; gaskets and seals 15 to 30 years, depending on cleaning

fig 4

fig 5

4. Glass wall;
5. Interior view

19

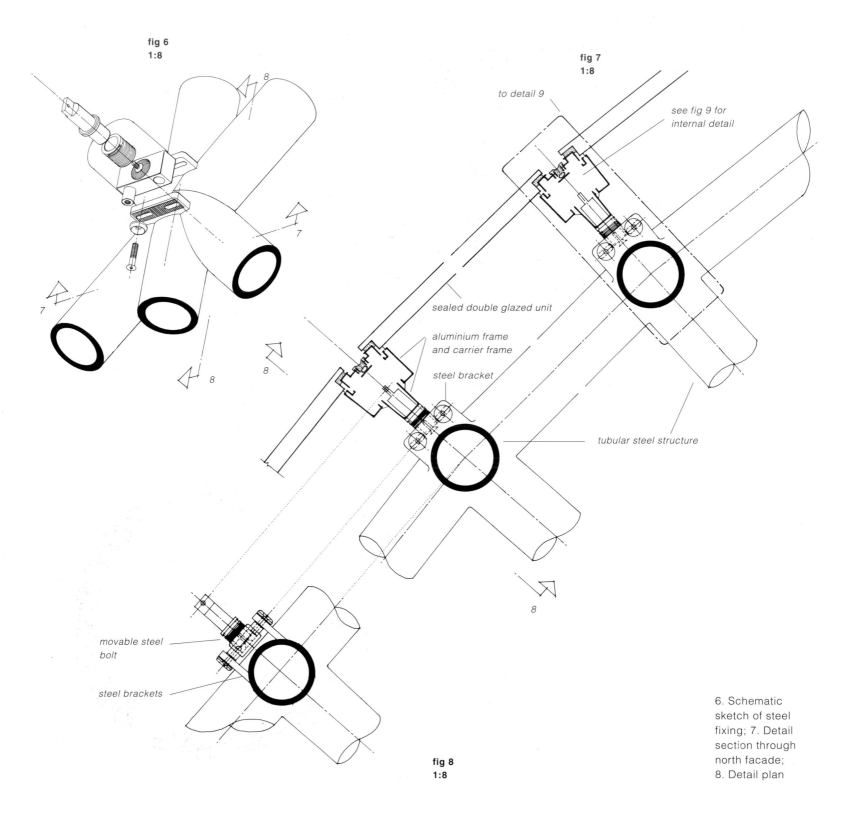

fig 6
1:8

fig 7
1:8

to detail 9

see fig 9 for
internal detail

sealed double glazed unit

aluminium frame
and carrier frame

steel bracket

tubular steel structure

8

8

7

7

8

8

movable steel
bolt

steel brackets

fig 8
1:8

6. Schematic
sketch of steel
fixing; 7. Detail
section through
north facade;
8. Detail plan

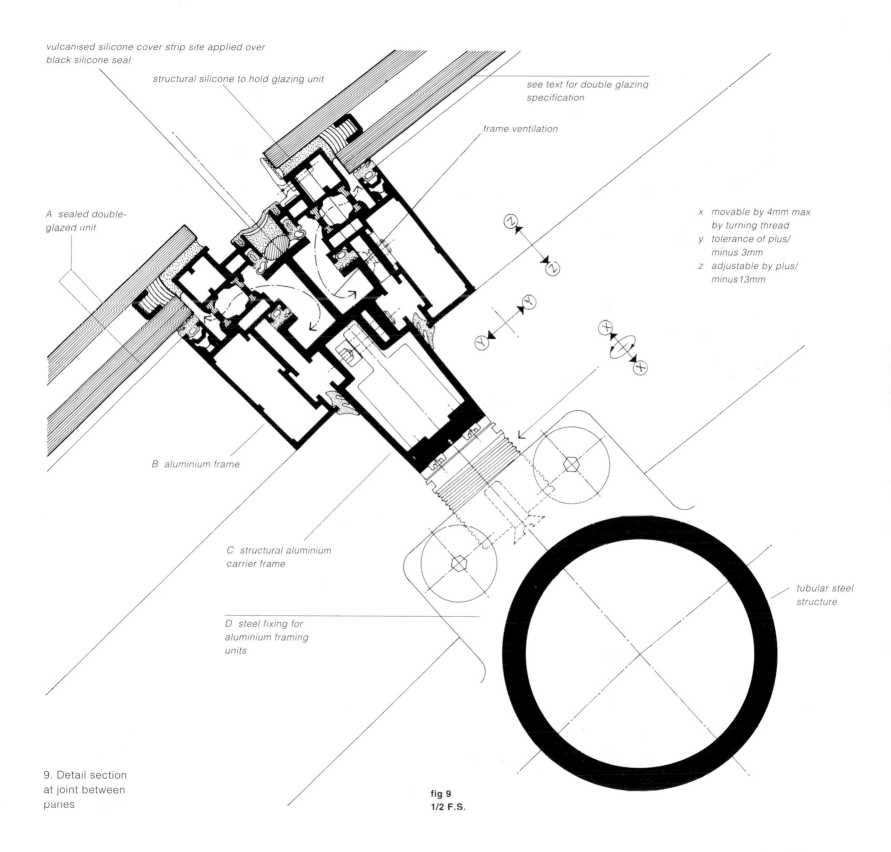

vulcanised silicone cover strip site applied over
black silicone seal

structural silicone to hold glazing unit

see text for double glazing
specification

frame ventilation

A sealed double-
glazed unit

x movable by 4mm max
   by turning thread
y tolerance of plus/
   minus 3mm
z adjustable by plus/
   minus 13mm

B aluminium frame

C structural aluminium
carrier frame

tubular steel
structure

D steel fixing for
aluminium framing
units

9. Detail section
at joint between
panes

fig 9
1/2 F.S.

fig 1

NICHOLAS GRIMSHAW & PARTNERS AND YRM ANTHONY HUNT ASSOCIATES

WATERLOO INTERNATIONAL RAIL TERMINAL

London

Brief

British Rail required a building to accommodate the new Eurostar terminal to the west of the main Waterloo station. The enclosure had to be 400 metres long, the length of a Eurostar passenger train, and the narrowness of the space – especially towards the southern end where the overall width was only 33 metres – precluded the use of intermediate columns.

The plan shape was tightly constrained by the confines of the site and the turning radius of the incoming trains, producing the curved funnel-shape shown on figures 1 and 2.

The budget for the steel and glass canopy was £12 million (just under ten per cent of total building cost of £130 million) and the target completion date was May 1993.

Design Response

BR interviewed several firms of architects in March 1988 and appointed Nicholas Grimshaw & Partners overall designers in the same month. YRM Anthony Hunt Associates (who had already been involved in preliminary work on the project) were retained as structural engineers for the steel and glass roof.

The vault profile finally agreed upon is shown in figure 8. The canopy rises steeply along the western perimeter, where space is tight, with a shallower profile along the eastern perimeter. The eastern side of the vault is clad with metal sheeting interrupted by a strip of glazing over each truss while the western side is entirely glazed [figures 11, 12].

Structural Concept

The steel structure is best understood as a set of primary and secondary elements.

The *primary* elements are the 37 arched trusses spanning the railway tracks [figure 3]. Each arch consists of a long, gently-curved bowstring truss shown as A in figure 4, and a short, tightly-curved bowstring truss shown as B, with the reinforced concrete floor and track beds C acting as the tie beam. These elements are connected by hinge-joints to form a three-pin arch,[1] a form of construction that has the great advantage over a fixed arch of being able to accommodate large differential movements (both vertically and horizontally) without detrimental effect. Each of the trusses A and B can freely expand, contract or otherwise deform under load without transferring bending moments into the opposite truss or transfering turning moments into the floor.

Figure 7 demonstrates that:

• Bending moments are zero at the pin joints.

• The long-spanning truss A has a high bending sagging moment at its centre. It therefore required a structural profile as shown in figure 6, with compression members at the top and a tension chord at the bottom.

• The short-spanning truss B, acting in a manner opposite to A because of its more vertical inclination and tight radius, has a bending 'hogging' moment at the centre (a tendency to bend outwards). It therefore required a reversed structural profile as shown in figure 5, with tension chords at the top and a compression member at the bottom.

The structural form developed by YRM-AHA closely resembles the stress diagram, suggesting a highly efficient design. As the arch spans reduce from 48.5 metres at the north end of the vault to 32.7 metres at the south end [figure 3] the truss depths and widths are scaled down in proportion, as are the tube diameters. Structural sizes are hence kept visibly in proportion to the forces that must be resisted – a nice touch typical of the care that permeates every aspect of this design.

The *secondary* structure consists of a two-way grid of steel tubes. The transverse tubes, shown as D in figures 13 and 21, run in the same direction as the primary trusses, located between them at approximately 3.6 centres. The longitudinal tubes, shown as E, run the length of the vault, connecting and stabilising the primary trusses. They dip down to form a valley between each pair of trusses to allow for rainwater run-off as shown on figure 21.

Both the primary and the secondary structures, made generally from grade 50 circular hollow sections, are braced by solid tension rods. Those bracing the primary trusses are shown on figures 14 and 19; those bracing the secondary structure on the west side are shown on figure 9.

Visual order is imposed upon this cat's cradle of structural members by clear distinctions between primary structure (the trusses) and secondary structure (the tubular members between trusses); between compression members (large diameter tubes) and tension members (small diameter rods); and between structural members and claddings – the latter always carefully spaced away from the tubular steel structure to maintain their separate identity.

Allowance for Structural Movement

All structures must allow for movement. At Waterloo the problem was especially severe due to the variable nature of the substructure, the dynamic loads imposed by the 800-seat trains entering and leaving the station, and the springiness of the pin-jointed arches.

The substructure comprised a patchwork of old arches on the station site, a bridge over Westminster Bridge Road and old building foundations beyond that. Even after the installation of new foundations there remained several different types of supporting structure as shown in figure 2, each with its own stiffness and settlement characteristics.

The design of the new train shed structure had to allow for these variations while coping with complex dead and live loads from many sources:

• Ground heave and subsidence. The basement raft area between gridlines 5 and 17 was predicted to rise by 26 millimetres over a period of years following the removal of earlier heavy masonry structures, while an adjacent area only one metre away was predicted to sink by 20 millimetres in response to newly imposed loads.

• Slow contraction of the concrete platform structure as it cured over a five-year period.

• The weight of the 800-tonne passenger trains depressing the rail bed by up to 11 millimetres as they entered the terminal.

• Longitudinal forces exerted upon the rail bed as trains travelled along the curved track and braked to a halt, pushing the rail bed both sideways and forward.

• Expansion and contraction of all parts of the structure in response to thermal change.

• Deformation of the vault in response to wind, snow and other live loads acting on the steel and glass claddings.

The sum of these movements is catered for by a hierarchy of movement joints as follows:

• At the macro scale there are six expansion joints slicing through the structure at roughly 60- to 80-metre centres as shown in figure 3.

• At intermediate scale, between the expansion joints described above, the secondary members E on figures 13 and 21 have expansion/contraction joints at 50- to 60-centimetre centres. These take up inaccuracies of construction and assembly, absorb thermal expansion or contraction of the steelwork and supporting structure, and absorb movements below. They are designed to be almost invisible, taking the form of a small tube telescoping inside a larger tube. No such telescoping joints are required across the vault as all cross-vault movement is taken up by the free flexing of trusses A and B [figure 4] accompanied by slight rotations at the three pin joints.

• At the micro scale very careful provision has been made for the movement of individual cladding panels, as follows:

The strips of planar glazing above the eastern trusses [figure 12] lie above the steel structure [figure 19], are relatively immune to movements in the latter, and compressible silicone seals [figure 22] are all that are required to absorb the small interpane movements.

The framed glass panels hung beneath the western trusses [figure 11] require much more sophisticated solutions. First, during installation, the stainless steel arms to which the aluminium fins are fixed could be individually rotated to the desired angles and then locked [see arrow U in figure 10]. Second, the fins can pivot around their fixings at both ends [arrow V]; are additionally free to slide at one end [arrow W]; and have freedom to slide laterally [arrow X]. Third, the glass panels fixed to the fins can slide both vertically [arrow Y] and laterally [arrow Z].

Structural Connections

Wherever possible the joints in the steel structure were designed as simple single-pin connections. This allowed for quick and easy site connections, the possibility of some rotational adjustment to line up and level the frames, and the assimilation of subsequent structural movement under the dead and live loads noted above.

The large connections in the three-pin arch [figure 4] are formed of A4 grade steel castings, cast in Zircon sand to give a quality finish, with 100-millimetre diameter stainless steel pins. Each casting consists mostly of solid metal, allowing the local forces brought to bear on the joint by a convergence of compression tubes and tension rods to flow smoothly round the joint and through the pin to the supporting structure. These castings were first modelled three-dimensionally by computer, then mocked up in expanded polystyrene and discussed with the casting contractor Noel Village Ltd, and were finally shaped as wooden patterns to make the sand moulds. Nodal connections within the bowstring trusses [figures 14,19] were modelled, tested and cast in the same manner.

Glazing Design

On the fully glazed west side of the vault, over-lapping panes of aluminium-framed glass are held between extruded aluminium fins suspended from the steel structure [figures 11, 14]. Using a conventional glazing system the doubly curved, diminishing-radius vault surface may well have needed over a thousand different pane shapes and sizes. To avoid such extravagance the design team adopted the overlapping pane system seen in figures 17 and 18 which allows considerable variation of pane size along the curve of the vault. Glass-to-glass joints along the curve of the vault are sealed by neoprene blades [figure 17] which allow the upper pane to move freely in relation to the one below. In the other direction, along the length of the vault [figure 18] the panes lie in the same plane but are well separated, again allowing considerable variation of pane size, and glass-to-glass joints are sealed by concertina-profile neoprene extrusions allowing lateral movement.

On the east side of the vault, glazing occurs only over each arched truss [figure 9] and consists of butt-jointed planar glazing with silicone seals [figure 22].

Contract

This had to be a fast-track project and Bovis Construction Ltd acted as construction managers for the terminal, allowing the design to be developed while the early construction packages were already under way on site. Due to the complexity of the roof design it was among the first to be let, despite being one of the last to be constructed.

Construction Process

The primary trusses A and B [figure 8] were assembled in the workshop by Westbury Tubular Structures Ltd on specially constructed jigs to ensure accuracy of the curved profiles. Once the basic members had been welded in place, the semi-complete trusses were lifted from the jig and moved to a separate area of the workshop, allowing welding of the tubular members to be completed while the next truss was placed on the jig. When welding of the tubular compression members was complete, the threaded-end diagonal ties were installed and finger-tightened to the correct length.

To test the system, an entire bay of steelwork was pre-erected by Westbury Tubular Structures Ltd. This was then clad by Briggs Amasco Ltd, the metal and glass cladding contractors. Only minor design modifications were needed as a result.

With regard to on-site erection, the major trusses A were transported to the site in three sections and the minor trusses B in one piece. Steelwork assembly started in two locations – on gridlines 1 and 17 – and proceeded southwards one bay at a time, with an average construction time of two to three weeks per bay, depending on complexity and other factors.

Paint System

All steelwork was shot-blasted, followed by an aluminium metal spray, etch primer and application of a multi-coat micaceous iron oxide paint system. A total of five coats was applied, giving a dry film thickness of 2.75 millimetres with a design life of 25 years to first maintenance.

Cleaning and Maintenance

British Rail required that all maintenance work must be able to proceed without disrupting the operation of the station. The steel and glass roof is therefore designed to take decked-out platforms suspended from the roof.

Conclusion

In contrast to the Leipzig Entrance Hall [pages 36-49] – which takes the form of a glass shell of maximum transparency and utter smoothness with all supports (except for four steel pins per pane) kept completey clear of the vault

– the vault at Waterloo is a crinkly, delicately ribbed steel-and-glass caterpillar whose character and visual density changes with each viewpoint.

Architecturally, as Peter Davey observes in the *Architectural Review* of September 1993 (pages 18-44), a walk along this interior offers 'one of the most moving and dramatic experiences in the history of glass and metal buildings'.

Technically the design is especially notable for the success with which standardised components and a single family of castings have been applied to a range of structural connections and many different glazing conditions. Only 229 pane types were applied to 1,680 glazing positions representing a great variety of field sizes and relative movement conditions. This was made possible by introducing an isolating 'movement zone' between all claddings and their supporting frames, consisting of the sliding connections shown in figures 17 and 18.

Notes

1 This is a structural form which many architectural students will recognise from the image of the 1889 Halle des Machines in *Space, Time and Architecture* by Sigfried Giedion, *The Sources of Modern Architecture and Design* by Nikolaus Pevsner, and other standard texts. Another memorable example was the 1909 AEG Turbine Hall in Berlin by Peter Behrens, where the pin joints are visible at the column bases.

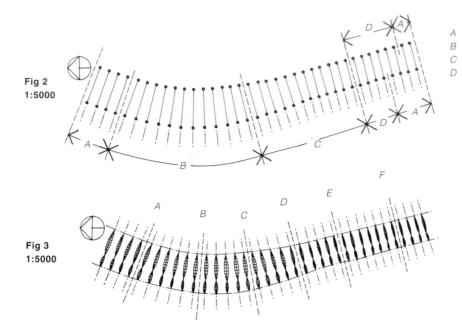

A   EXISTING BRICK ARCHES
B   NEW TERMINAL BASEMENT
C   EXISTING MODIFIED BRICK ARCHES
D   GIRDER

Fig 2
1:5000

2. Substructure

Fig 3
1:5000

3. Positions of
expansion joints

SUMMARY DATA

Client:

European Passenger Services, British Rail

Timetable:

Design commenced March 1988; demolition commenced December 1990; steel frame erection commenced October 1991; steel frame erection completed October 1992; glazing commenced November 1991; glazing completed November 1992; overall building completed May 1993

Architects:

Nicholas Grimshaw & Partners, London

Structural design:

YRM Anthony Hunt Associates, Cirencester

Quantity Surveyor:

Davis Langdon & Everest, London

Project Manager:

Bovis Construction Ltd, London

Roof cladding and glazing contractor:

Briggs Amasco, London

Steelwork fabricator:

Westbury Tubular Structures Ltd, Wetherby

Castings fabricators:

Cronite Precision Castings Ltd, Crewkerne; Holbrook Precision Castings Ltd, Sheffield; Noel Village Ltd, Rotherham

Glass manufacturer:

Pilkington UK Ltd, St Helens

Developed glass area:

2.5 acres

Weight of steel:

1,100 tonnes

Number and specification of clear glass panes:

1,680 panes of 10mm-thick toughened glass, comprising 229 different pane sizes

Glazing seals:

West side of roof: neoprene seals as shown on figures 17 and 18. East side of roof: silicone seals as shown on figure 22

Total cost (final):

£13.6 million at 1989 prices

Life expectancy:

Canopy overall:125 years with minimal maintenance; paint system: 25 years to first maintenance

Fig 4

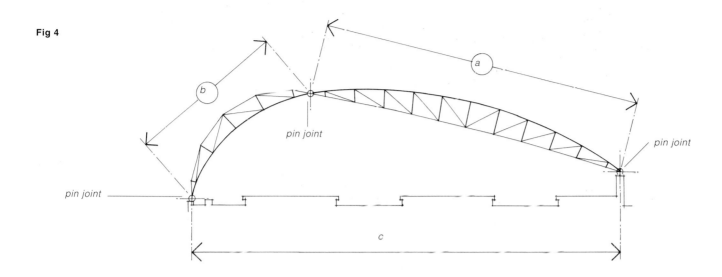

b

a

pin joint

pin joint

pin joint

c

Fig 5

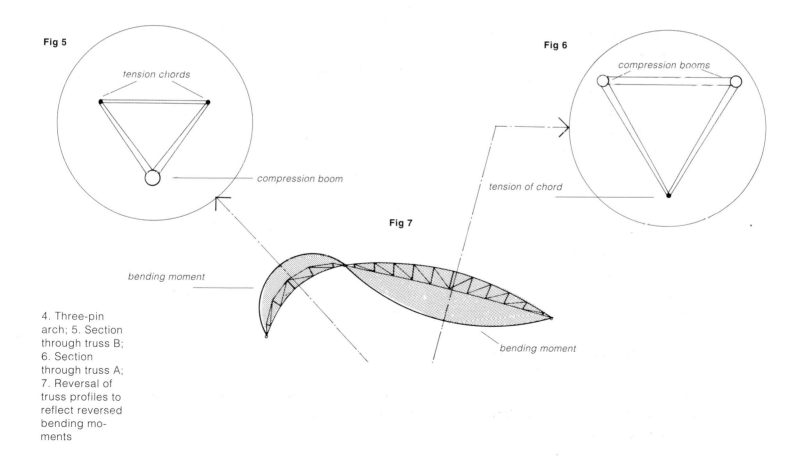

tension chords

compression boom

Fig 6

compression booms

tension of chord

Fig 7

bending moment

bending moment

4. Three-pin arch; 5. Section through truss B; 6. Section through truss A; 7. Reversal of truss profiles to reflect reversed bending moments

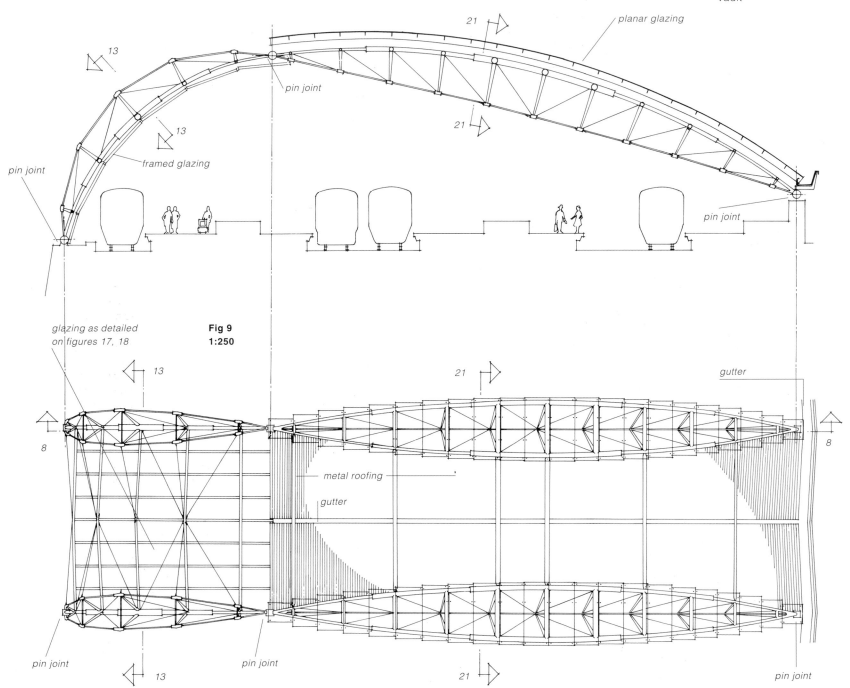

Fig 8
1:250

8. Cross section looking in the opposite direction to figure 20;
9. Plan of bay at northern end of vault

planar glazing

pin joint

framed glazing

pin joint

pin joint

13

13

21

21

glazing as detailed on figures 17, 18

Fig 9
1:250

gutter

13

metal roofing

gutter

8

8

pin joint

pin joint

pin joint

13

21

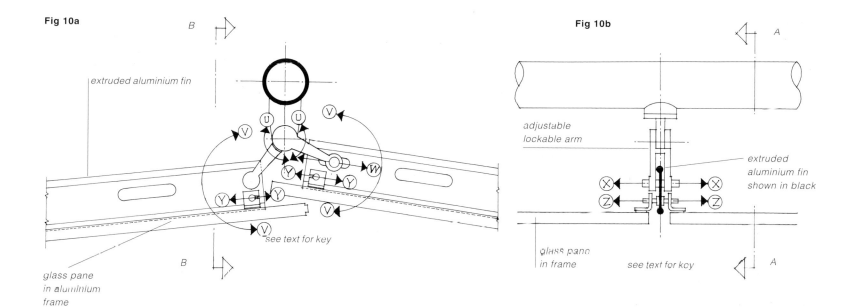

Fig 10a

extruded aluminium fin

B

B

see text for key

glass pane in aluminium frame

Fig 10b

A

A

adjustable lockable arm

extruded aluminium fin shown in black

glass pane in frame

see text for key

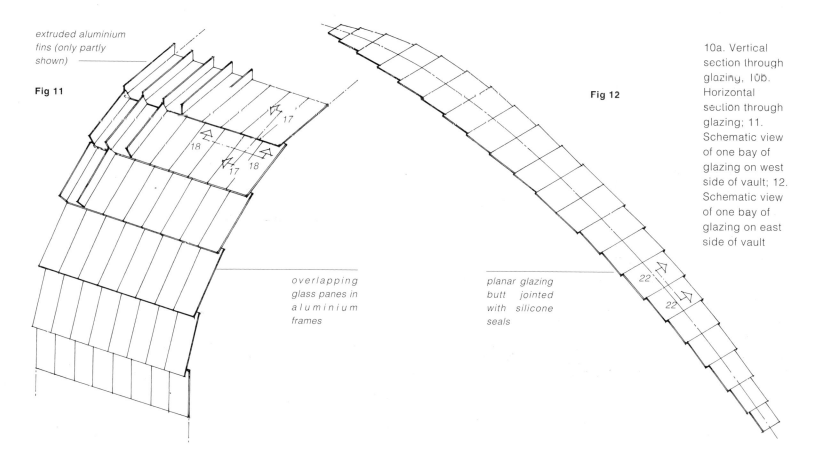

extruded aluminium fins (only partly shown)

Fig 11

overlapping glass panes in aluminium frames

Fig 12

planar glazing butt jointed with silicone seals

10a. Vertical section through glazing, 10b. Horizontal section through glazing; 11. Schematic view of one bay of glazing on west side of vault; 12. Schematic view of one bay of glazing on east side of vault

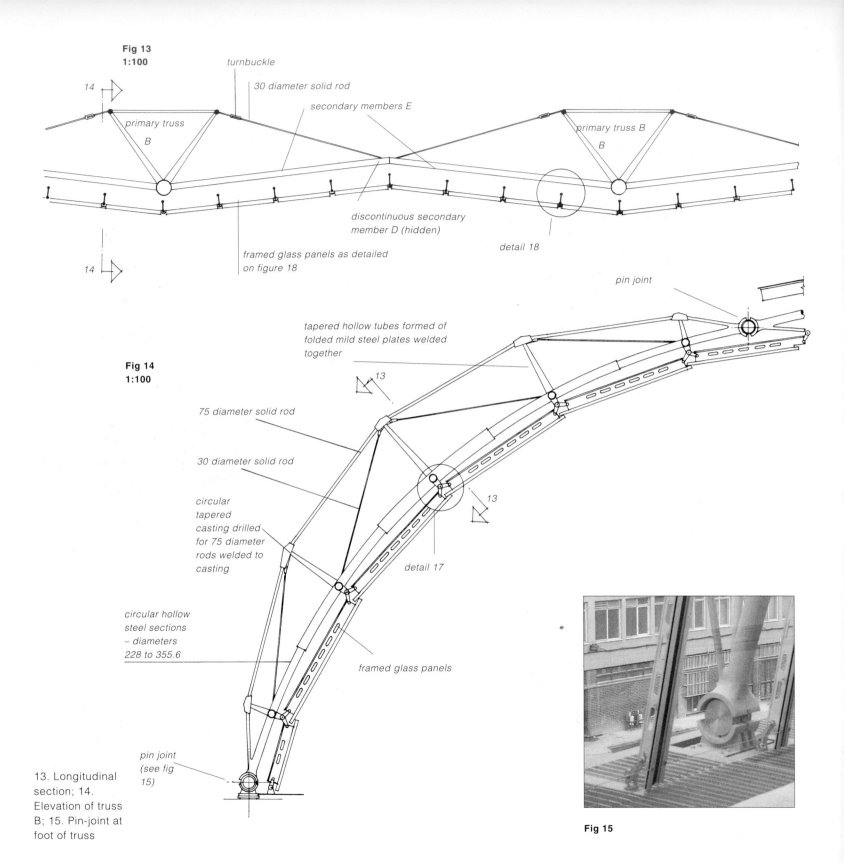

Fig 13
1:100

14

turnbuckle

30 diameter solid rod

secondary members E

primary truss
B

primary truss B
B

discontinuous secondary
member D (hidden)

detail 18

framed glass panels as detailed
on figure 18

14

pin joint

tapered hollow tubes formed of
folded mild steel plates welded
together

Fig 14
1:100

13

75 diameter solid rod

30 diameter solid rod

circular
tapered
casting drilled
for 75 diameter
rods welded to
casting

13

detail 17

circular hollow
steel sections
– diameters
228 to 355.6

framed glass panels

pin joint
(see fig
15)

13. Longitudinal
section; 14.
Elevation of truss
B; 15. Pin-joint at
foot of truss

Fig 15

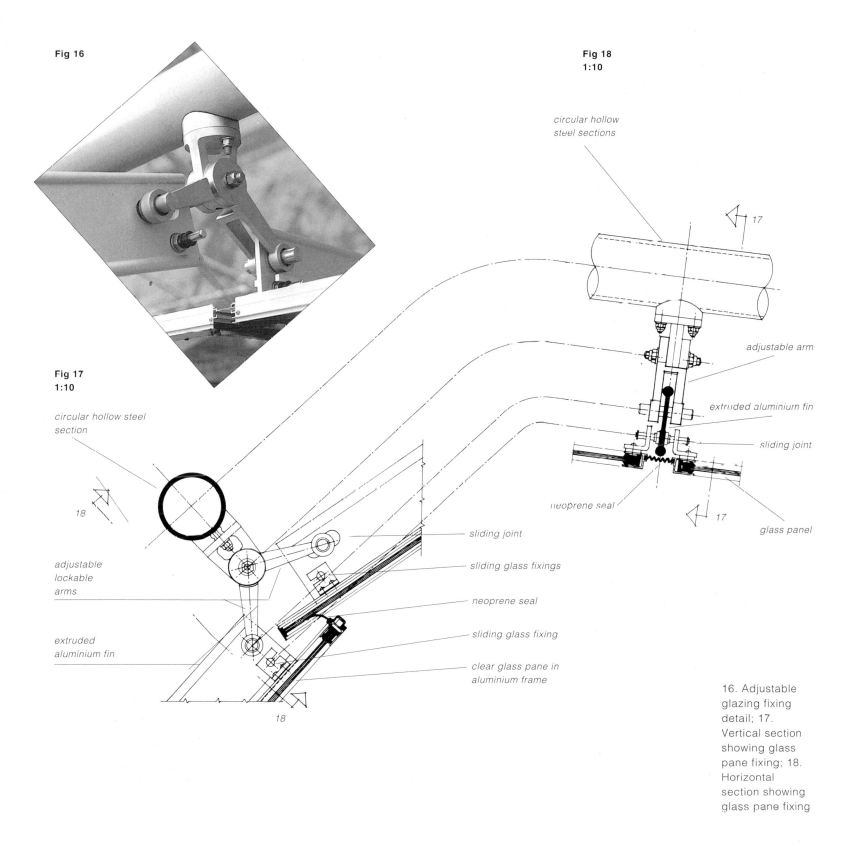

Fig 16

Fig 18
1:10

circular hollow
steel sections

17

adjustable arm

extruded aluminium fin

sliding joint

neoprene seal

17

glass panel

Fig 17
1:10

circular hollow steel
section

18

adjustable
lockable
arms

extruded
aluminium fin

sliding joint

sliding glass fixings

neoprene seal

sliding glass fixing

*clear glass pane in
aluminium frame*

18

16. Adjustable
glazing fixing
detail; 17.
Vertical section
showing glass
pane fixing; 18.
Horizontal
section showing
glass pane fixing

Fig 19
1:100

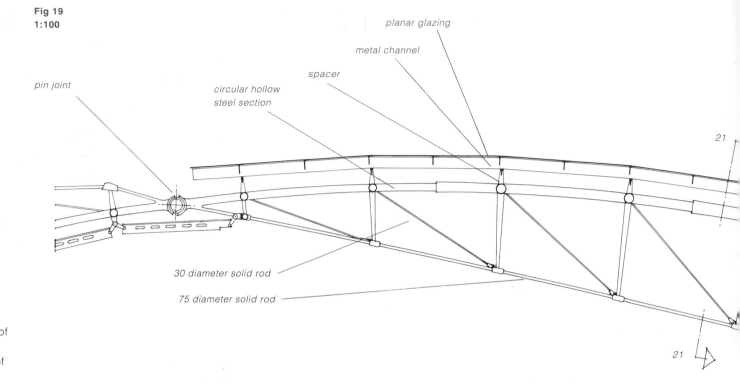

pin joint

circular hollow
steel section

spacer

planar glazing

metal channel

21

30 diameter solid rod

75 diameter solid rod

21

19. Elevation of
truss A; 20.
Interior view of
the platform
(looking in the
opposite direc-
tion to elevations
14 and 19); 21.
Section through
truss A; 22.
Glass cladding
over truss A

Fig 20

Fig 21
1:100

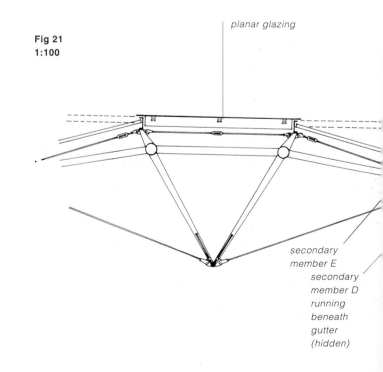

planar glazing

secondary
member E
secondary
member D
running
beneath
gutter
(hidden)

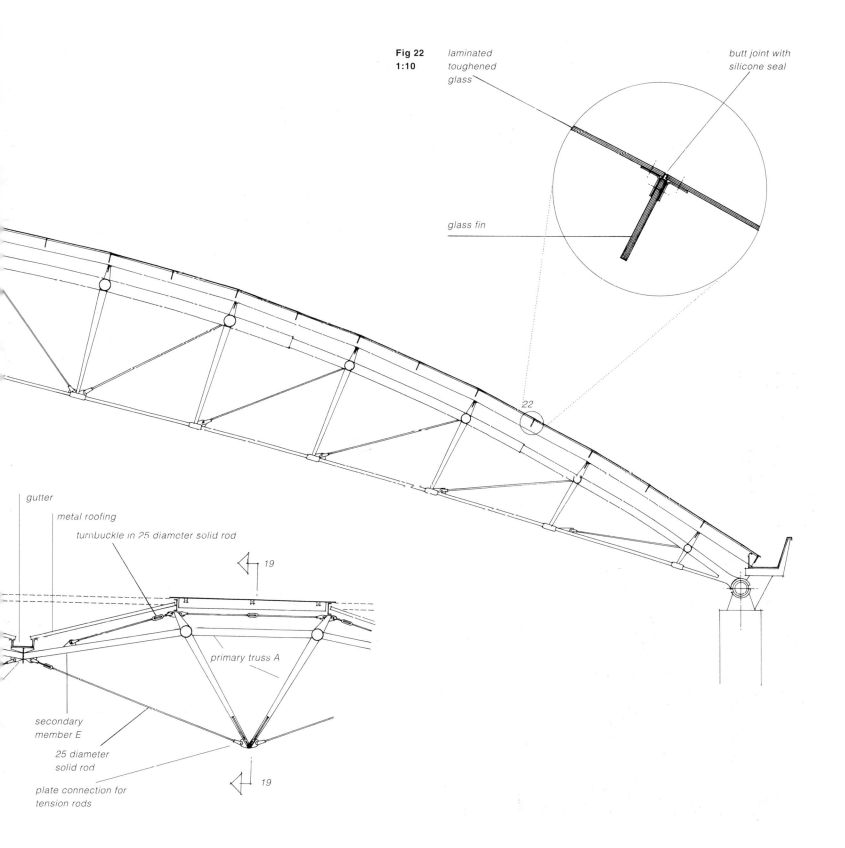

Fig 22
1:10

laminated toughened glass

butt joint with silicone seal

glass fin

22

gutter

metal roofing

turnbuckle in 25 diameter solid rod

19

primary truss A

secondary member E

25 diameter solid rod

plate connection for tension rods

19

Fig 1

VON GERKAN, MARG & PARTNERS AND IAN RITCHIE ARCHITECTS

CENTRAL ENTRANCE HALL EXHIBITION AND CONFERENCE CENTRE

Leipzig, Germany

Leipzig, a centre of trade fairs for over 800 years, has developed a new exhibition and conference centre comprising more than 100,000sqm of useful hall space at an overall cost of 1.3 billion DM. A glazed central entrance that gives access to the main exhibition halls [figure 1] was completed in 1996. It is an innovative and elegant example of a transparent and, on its inner face, completely smooth-surfaced glass enclosure.

Brief

The requirement was for a clear-span hall approximately 244 metres long, 80 metres across and 30 metres high. A light, transparent enclosure was favoured and the budget set at 90 million DM. A preliminary design was prepared by Von Gerkan, Marg and Partners. In November 1992 Ian Ritchie Architects were invited to join the team and help develop an improved design to a reduced budget.

Concept Design

Ian Ritchie Architects proposed a prefabricated steel-and-glass structure offering:
- An ultra-light and transparent appearance.
- A construction cost within the new budget of 65 million DM.
- The possibility of vault assembly proceeding in parallel with concreting operations below.
- Complete demountability of both the steel and glass structures.

Following the design philosophy outlined on page 13, the team evolved a structural concept consisting of three clearly separated hierarchical layers. In descending order of scale these are:

Primary system: ten trussed arches, shown as A on figure 4, form the outer layer. These arches have no loadbearing function and merely stabilise the tubular steel shell (a role that would normally be performed by crosswalls, an option ruled out in this case to avoid compromising the clarity of the vaulted space) but their over-arching positions make them visually dominant. Truss depth varies from 4 metres at the apex to 10 metres where the truss meets the ground [figure 4]. Here the upper chord spans across the service road on each side of the hall, anchoring the composition into the landscape. Construction throughout is hot-dip galvanised mild steel tubing, bolted together for demountability and painted silver-grey.

Secondary steel shell: a curved shell, shown as B, formed of 3.125 x 3.125 metre cells. Again, the construction is hot-dip galvanised mild steel tubing, bolted together for demountability and painted silver-grey. To maintain a neutral grid

1. Central Entrance Hall Exhibition and Conference Centre, Leipzig

texture there is no cross-bracing; all bolt connections are invisibly formed inside the tubes; and tube external diameters are kept constant, local variations of load being catered for by varying the tube wall thickness rather than tube diameter. Thermal expansion and contraction along the 244-metre length of the vault (which may be as much as 120 millimetres overall) are absorbed not by the usual method of movement joints, which would have been visually disruptive, but by supporting the steel shell on dense neoprene blocks which allow the shell to move along the longitudinal axis.

Glass shell: Suspended beneath the steel grid is the least assertive of the three layers – a thin and highly transparent glass membrane shown as C in figure 4.

All three elements are brought right down to ground level so that people can form a direct tactile relationship with the lofty structure by touching and experiencing all the elements that are distantly seen overhead. It comes as quite a surprise, for instance, to realise that the frogfingers are not the tiny spiderlike objects they may seem in remote silhouette [figure 1] but hefty metal castings of pleasing mass and texture.

Glass Shell Design

A fixing method was required that would:

• Hold the glass panes securely in position.

• Give a completely smooth interior surface.

• Allow maximum transparency. Analysis of earlier glass structures designed by Ian Ritchie Architects had established that a pronounced sense of transparency depends on the total area covered by solid structure not exceeding 15 per cent of the total area. The design requirements were therefore: (a) to design a support system that would leave at least 85 per cent of the glass surface unobstructed to radial views out; and (b) to choose a vault form ensuring that the glass surface was always roughly perpendicular to the line of sight for people looking out, to limit the effect of structural intrusion and perceived reflections.

• Allow for deformation (both in the surface plane and perpendicular to it) in the steel structure and in the glass membrane hung from it, due to load and thermal movements.

The system that was developed is illustrated in figures 6 to16.

Each glass pane of approximately 3.1 x 1.5 metres is held by four stainless steel suspension bolts as shown in figures 16 and 29. The steel structure deforms relatively more than the glass, and spherical bearings in the glass plane [figures 26-28] are incorporated in all suspension bolts to avoid the transfer of bending stresses into the glass. To allow for free in-plane movement of the glass sheet in all directions only one of the four suspension bolts is fixed [figure 28]. The second bolt is pivoted to allow movement along the long axis of the pane, and the remaining two have universal joints to allow for movement along both axes of the pane. The heads of the suspension bolts are virtually flush with the internal glass surface.

As shown in sections 12 and 14 the suspension bolts are fixed to frogfingers which in turn are bolted to the arched members of the tubular steel grid above. During site assembly the angles of the frogfinger arms could be individually screw-adjusted [arrows X in figure 18] and the positions of the glass fixings adjusted both vertically [arrows Y] and horizontally [arrows Z].

The glass panes are laminated for safety. Nearly 50 different destructive tests were conducted on trial panes to prove their ability to maintain structural integrity under all loadings.

Joints between glass panes are completely weathertight. They are formed of silicone profiles [figures 13, 15] which allow for 8 millimetres of movement in any direction. The stepped glass edges give a secure seating for the two-part sealing system and allow sealing operations to be carried out from the outside.

Allowance for Structural Movement

There are two sources of movement – (a) expansion and contraction due to temperature change and (b) structural deformation due to wind and snow loads. These interact in a complex manner to produce two kinds of movement in both the steel and glass structures – out-of-plane [for instance as in figure 19] and in-plane [for instance as in figure 20].

Out-of-plane movement causes the steel grid to deflect locally by up to 8 millimetres. This is easily dealt with: the glass membrane absorbs movements by hingelike deformation of the flexible silicone pane-to-pane joints [figure 19].

In-plane movement is mainly due to thermally-induced expansion and contraction of the steel and glass structures along the longitudinal axis of the vault, which could total

250 millimetres The coefficients of movement are different for the two materials, resulting in differential movement between steel and glass of as much as 125 millimetres over the length of the vault. This must be absorbed by the glass fixings without inducing any bending stresses into the glass. The solution to the problem is twofold. First the elasticity of the silicone pane-to-pane joints [figures 22, 23] allow this movement to be evenly distributed throughout the length of the glass vault, thus reducing the amount of differential movement at any particular point; then the resultant differential movement at each fixing point is absorbed by the pivoting glass suspension bolts [figure 29].

Construction Process

The first of the three 'layers of construction' to be erected was the tubular steel shell [figure 7]. This was erected in a ladder-like fashion: the grid was bolted together on the ground in units measuring roughly 9.5 x 12.0 metres and hoisted up into position as shown in figure 32. After completion of each individual segment of the vault, the geometrical shape was corrected using jigs, and the connection bolts prestressed.

After completion of each 25-metre length of tubular steel vaulting [figure 33] the trussed arch for that bay was erected, starting with the bottom chord and continuing up from the base.

Finally the glass membrane [figure 10] was assembled. To fit the panes in position, the erection contractors Seele GmbH devised an electrically driven trolley, travelling along the outer radius of the vault on temporary rails to take each pane to its precise fixing location. The vault was glazed segment by segment, starting always at the top and working down [figure 34] in the following manner:

• A number of panes, prefitted with their stainless steel suspension bolts, were clamped to the trolley.

• On arrival at the first fixing location the trolley stopped, with the glass panes held immediately beneath the fixing points.

• One glass pane was then unclamped from the trolley, raised to the waiting frogfingers already bolted to the tubular steel grid, and bolt-fixed to the frogfingers [figure 36].

• The trolley unclamped itself, drove to the next fixing position, and repeated the process.

The tempered-glass panes could not be cut to fit the actual on-site dimensions of the tubular steel cells, which might vary up to 3 millimetres from the specified size of 3.125 x 3.125. The design therefore allowed three kinds of adjustment to be made as the glass fixing proceeded. First, as the frogfingers were being bolted to the tubular steel grid, they could be slightly rotated to correct for local deviations in the steelwork [X in figure 18]. Second, as the panes were fixed to the frogfingers, in-plane adjustments could be made via oversized holes in the plate connections between fixing bolts and frogfingers [Z in figure 18]. Third, as the panes were fixed to the frogfingers, out-of-plane adjustments could be made by screw-adjusting the lengths of the suspension bolts [Y in figure 18].

In this way 5,687 panes were accurately mounted in seven months. The hall was completed at less than budget cost and within the target completion date.

Environmental Control

High ventilation rates can be achieved via continuous inlet venting along the base of the vault and outlet venting at the crown (both computer-controlled), and further cooling can be obtained by irrigating the glass roof. Solar heat gain is reduced by partial fritting of the glass on the south side of the vault, high enough to be above normal sightlines. Local shading by large umbrellas and sunshades further reduces perceived temperature in occupied areas within the hall.

Cleaning and Maintenance

Externally, a robot runs along the crown of the building and winches itself up and down the curved surface, so washing the glass. Internally, mobile towers are brought into the hall via 5 x 4.5 metre-high glazed vehicle doors.

Servicing

Each primary arch [figure 4] is equipped with an access way, water and electrical supply. In addition a set of external bridge gantries span the upper half of the structure and can run on rails along the full length of the building, passing between the tubular steel shell and the lower chord of the primary trusses.

Inside the vault there is a regular grid of suspension points, flush with the inner glass surface, for hanging exhibits. Each point can carry up to 500 kilogrammes.

SUMMARY DATA

Client:

Leipzig Messe GmbH

Timetable:

Design competition: October 1992; construction commenced August 1994; completion: December 1995; opening: April 1996

Overall design:

Von Gerkan, Marg and Partners, Hamburg

Glass shell design:

Ian Ritchie Architects, London

Structural Engineers:

Polonyi & Partners, Cologne, with assistance to Ian Ritchie Architects from Ove Arup and Partners, London

Main contractors:

Mero Raumstruktur GmbH, Würzburg. Glasbau Seele GmbH, Gersthofen

Glass manufacture:

PPG Starphire, Perry, Georgia

Floor area:

19,520sqm

Glazed area:

26,050sqm

Area of fritted panes:

5,687sqm

Number of ventilation louvres:

142

Weight of steel:

2,070 tonnes

Weight of glass:

1,140 tonnes

Number and specification of clear glass panes:

5,526 panes [figure 29] weighing 190 kg each. Each pane is a 3.105 x 1.524 metre sandwich that is 18mm thick, and made of two 8mm safety glass outer sheets laminated to a core of two 0.76mm pvb layers [figures 13, 15]. Both outer sheets are low-iron glass ('white glass') which is free of the greenish cast characteristic of standard glass

Number and specification of frogfingers:

9,800 hot-dip galvanised cast carbon steel frogfingers of 28kg each, finished in the same silver-grey paint as the tubular structure [figures 12, 14]

Number and specification of suspension points:

22,500 machined stainless steel adjustable suspension bolts with internal ball joint to prevent bending stresses entering the glass panes [figures 26-28]. To avoid electrolytic interaction between the carbon steel frogfingers and stainless steel suspension bolts they are separated by dense polymer washers

Length and specification jointing:

25,000 linear metres of multicomponent jointing consisting of (a) prefabricated U-profile silicone strip to absorb up to 8mm of interpane movement, plus (b) silicone mastic to seal the joint to the glass. See figures 13 and 15

Total cost:

65,000,000 DM; cost/sqm of floor area: 3,330 DM/sqm

Glazing timetable:

7 months using 50 part-time installers

Life expectancy:

Canopy overall: approx 100 years; silicone joints: 20-30 years with regular washing

Fig 2

Fig 3
1:100

A   *TUBULAR STEEL TRUSSED ARCHES SPACED 25
METRES ON CENTRE*
B   *CURVED GRID OF STEEL TUBES – SEE FIGURE 7*
C   *GLASS SHELL – SEE FIGURE 10*

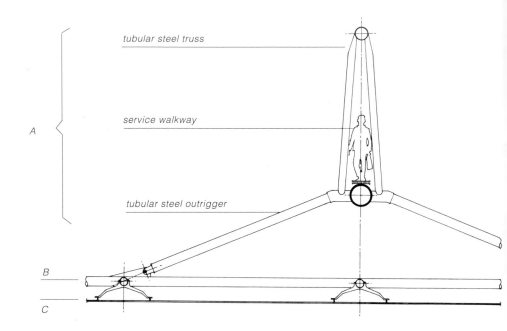

tubular steel truss

A

service walkway

tubular steel outrigger

B

C

2. Close-up of
the roof; 3.
Enlarged part-
elevation
showing truss
and outriggers;
4. Cross section;
5. Part-elevation

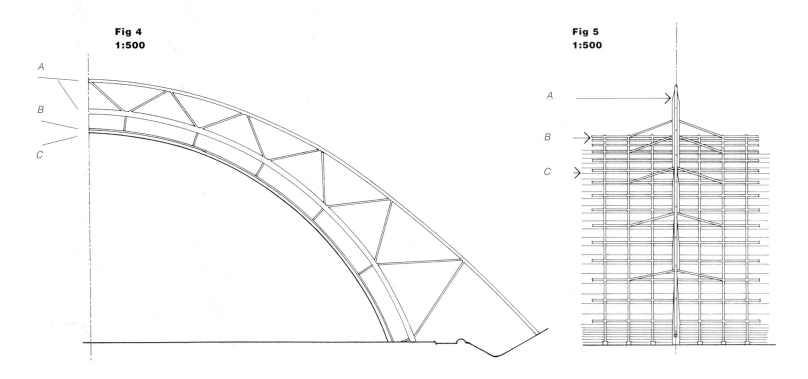

Fig 4
1:500

A

B

C

Fig 5
1:500

A

B

C

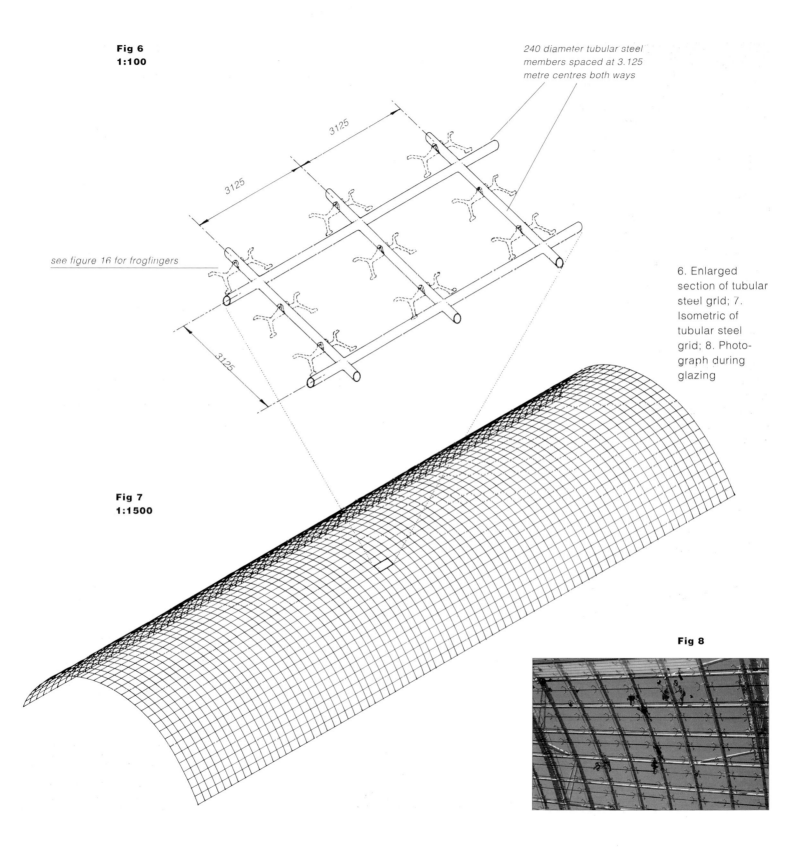

Fig 6
1:100

240 diameter tubular steel members spaced at 3.125 metre centres both ways

3125

3125

see figure 16 for frogfingers

3125

6. Enlarged section of tubular steel grid; 7. Isometric of tubular steel grid; 8. Photograph during glazing

Fig 7
1:1500

Fig 8

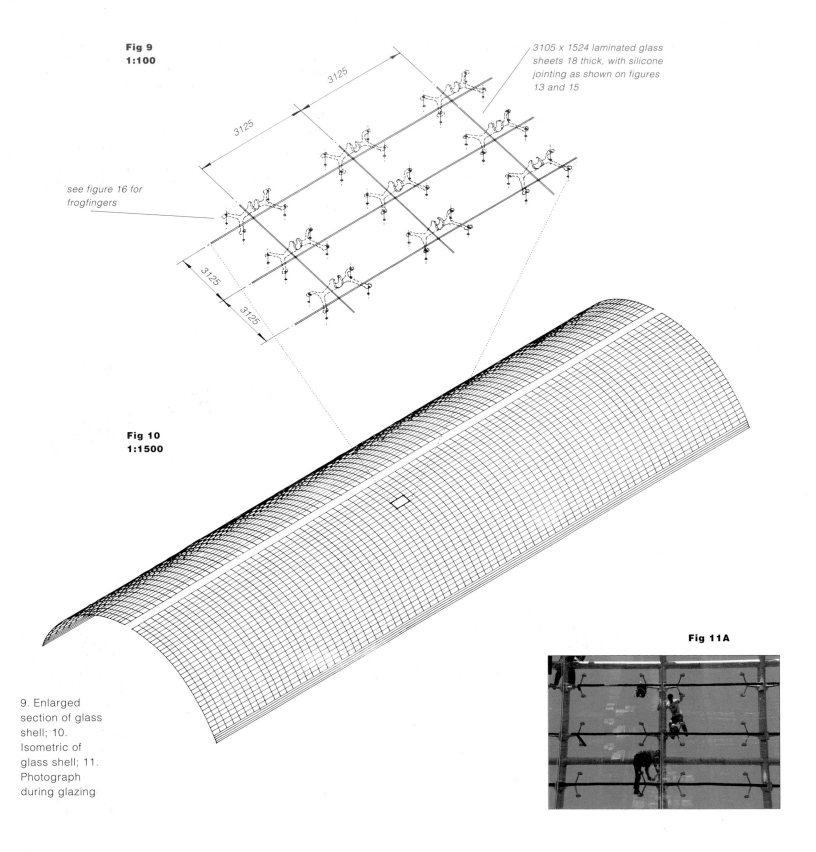

Fig 9
1:100

3125

3125

3125

3105 x 1524 laminated glass
sheets 18 thick, with silicone
jointing as shown on figures
13 and 15

see figure 16 for
frogfingers

3125

3125

Fig 10
1:1500

Fig 11A

9. Enlarged
section of glass
shell; 10.
Isometric of
glass shell; 11.
Photograph
during glazing

44

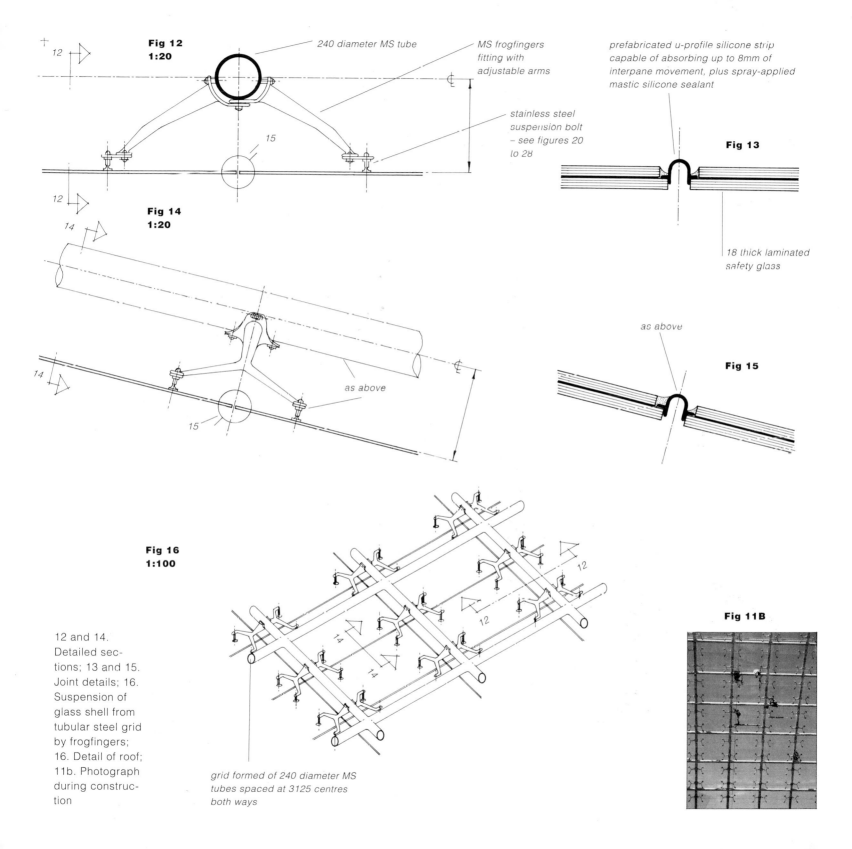

Fig 12
1:20

240 diameter MS tube

MS frogfingers fitting with adjustable arms

stainless steel suspension bolt – see figures 20 to 28

15

Fig 14
1:20

15

as above

prefabricated u-profile silicone strip capable of absorbing up to 8mm of interpane movement, plus spray-applied mastic silicone sealant

Fig 13

18 thick laminated safety glass

as above

Fig 15

Fig 16
1:100

12

12

14

14

Fig 11B

12 and 14. Detailed sections; 13 and 15. Joint details; 16. Suspension of glass shell from tubular steel grid by frogfingers; 16. Detail of roof; 11b. Photograph during construction

grid formed of 240 diameter MS tubes spaced at 3125 centres both ways

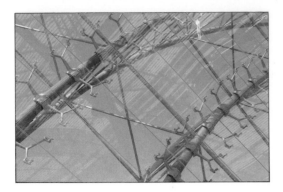

Fig 17

X   FROGFINGER ARMS MAY
     BE ROTATED BY SCREW-
     ADJUSTMENT
Y   STAINLESS STEEL
     SUSPENSION BOLT
     ALLOWS VERTICAL
     ADJUSTABILITY OF UP TO
     10mm
Z   SLIDING FIXINGS ALLOW
     LATERAL ADJUSTABILITY

Fig 18

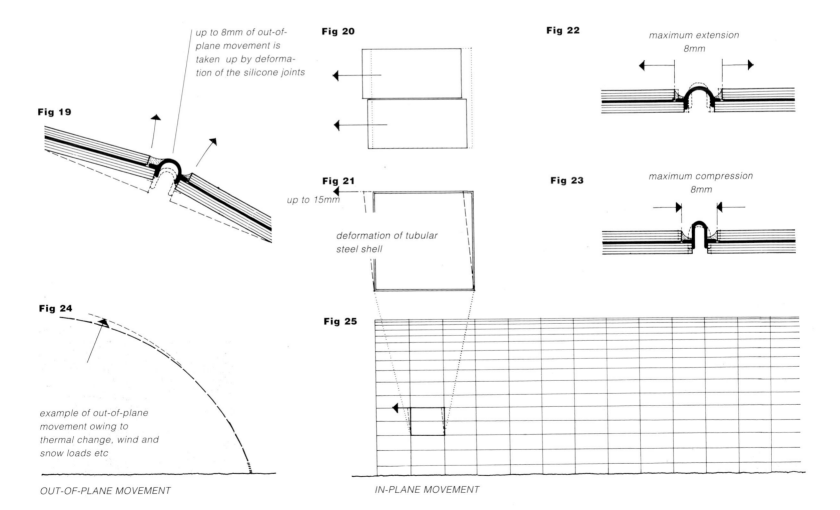

Fig 19

up to 8mm of out-of-plane movement is taken up by deformation of the silicone joints

Fig 20

Fig 21

up to 15mm

deformation of tubular steel shell

Fig 22

maximum extension 8mm

Fig 23

maximum compression 8mm

Fig 24

example of out-of-plane movement owing to thermal change, wind and snow loads etc

OUT-OF-PLANE MOVEMENT

Fig 25

IN-PLANE MOVEMENT

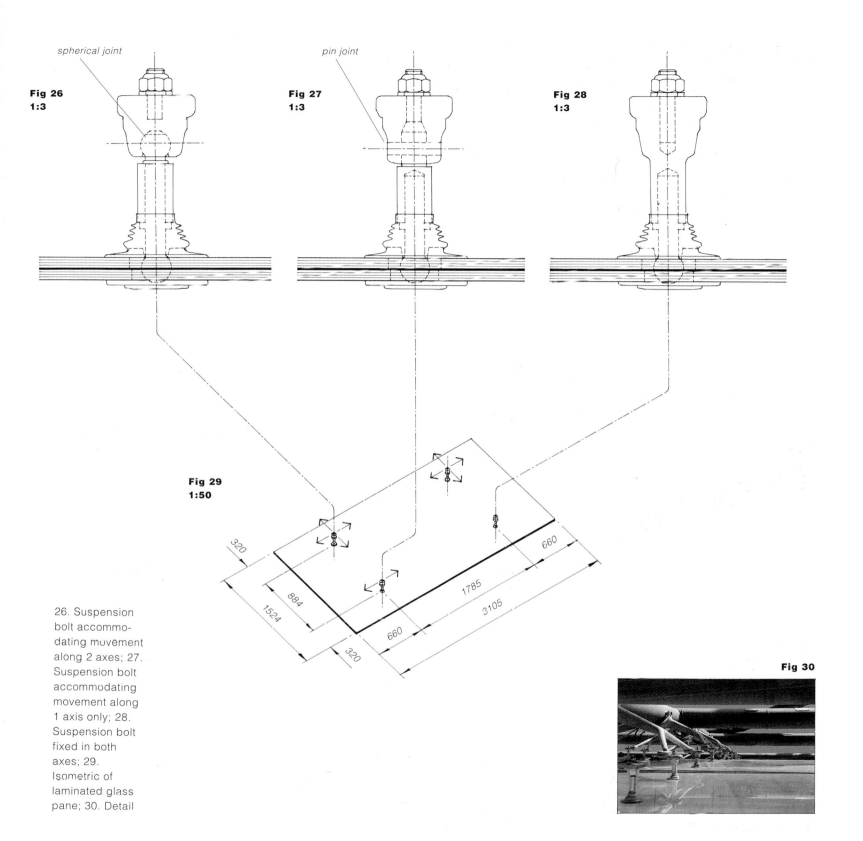

spherical joint

Fig 26
1:3

pin joint

Fig 27
1:3

Fig 28
1:3

Fig 29
1:50

320

660

1785

884

1524

3105

660

320

26. Suspension bolt accommodating movement along 2 axes; 27. Suspension bolt accommodating movement along 1 axis only; 28. Suspension bolt fixed in both axes; 29. Isometric of laminated glass pane; 30. Detail

Fig 30

Fig 31

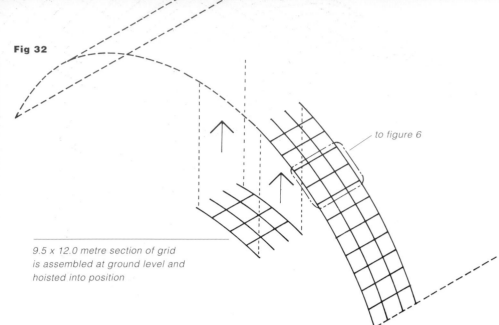

Fig 32

*9.5 x 12.0 metre section of grid
is assembled at ground level and
hoisted into position*

to figure 6

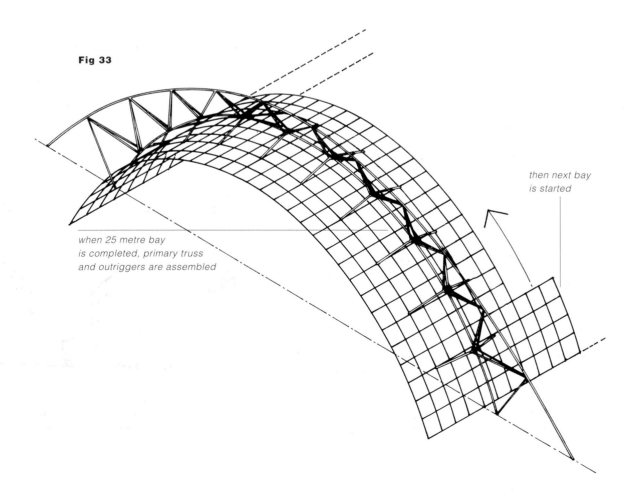

Fig 33

*when 25 metre bay
is completed, primary truss
and outriggers are assembled*

*then next bay
is started*

31. Detail of roof;
32. Erection of
tubular steel
grid; 33. Stabilis-
ing of completed
bay

Fig 34

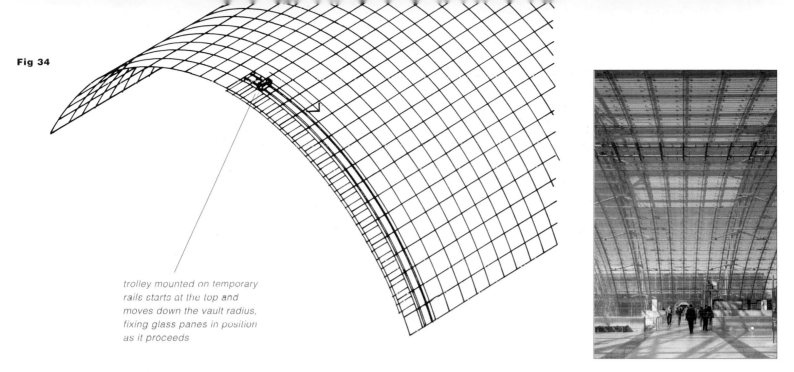

trolley mounted on temporary
rails starts at the top and
moves down the vault radius,
fixing glass panes in position
as it proceeds

Fig 35

Fig 36

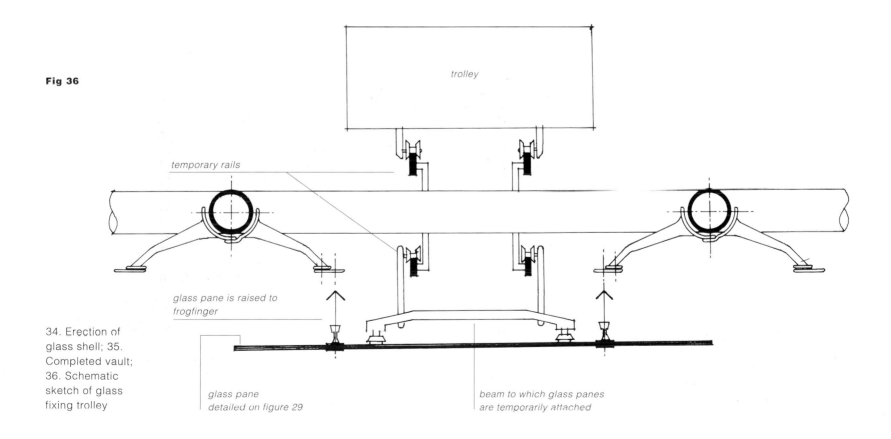

trolley

temporary rails

glass pane is raised to
frogfinger

glass pane
detailed on figure 29

beam to which glass panes
are temporarily attached

34. Erection of
glass shell; 35.
Completed vault;
36. Schematic
sketch of glass
fixing trolley

Fig 1

SIR MICHAEL HOPKINS & PARTNERS
AND OVE ARUP & PARTNERS

BRACKEN HOUSE ENTRANCE CANOPY

London

Bracken House in Friday Street, just to the south of St Paul's Cathedral, started life as the Financial Times printing works, designed by Sir Albert Richardson. In 1987 the FT moved out and the new owners commissioned Michael Hopkins & Partners to convert the neoclassical building to a modern office block. Hopkins' new design, the story of which is more fully told in the *Architectural Review* of May 1992 (pages 27-39), retained the two brickwork ends of Richardson's building but replaced the entire central area, providing new east and west street facades and a new entrance canopy.

Modern architects have a love affair with the idea of the ultra smooth glass skin from which all visible frameworks and fixings – and indeed all references to the force of gravity – have been abolished, leaving only magically suspended sheer glass. But at Bracken House Michael Hopkins chose the very opposite approach, enclosing an extremely sophisticated building within loadbearing facades harking back over a century to the 1865 Oriel Chambers in Liverpool.

The entrance canopy, in striking contrast with these toughly modelled dark facades, is a thin and icily cool plane of sheer glass. It is hung from a cat's cradle of supports, but its underside is completely smooth and free of fixings except for a single flat disc at the corner of each pane. To welcome the visitor and heighten the sense of lightness, a row of tiny lights sparkles along each joint, fed by fibre-optic conduits running invisibly in the stainless steel canopy ribs.

Structural Concept

As can be seen from figures 4 and 5, the canopy is hung from five steel rings, two fixed to the building frame at high level and three at a lower level. From these rings five sets of stainless steel tendons radiate downwards to support the nine tubular steel ribs of the glass canopy. Starting at the highest level (the five steel rings), and ending with the lowest (the glass shell), the structure is as follows.

The radiating steel tendons are connected to the upper rings by fork ends as shown in plan on figures 10 and 11. These tendons vary from about 21 to 38 millimetres in diameter and resist both tensile forces (eg downward loads due to snow or maintenance personnel) and compression forces (eg upward pressure caused by wind uplift). Each tendon has oppositely threaded ends and can be shortened or lengthened by rotating the central section as shown on figure 7, thus enabling the entire structure to be periodically re-tuned.

1. Bracken
House Entrance
Canopy, London

Connected to the lower ends of the tendons are five canopy ribs, each a stainless steel tube to which several attachments are welded [figure 8]:

• Welded to the top are four holed fixing lugs, enabling the rib to be connected to the overhead tendons via ring connectors as shown on plan in figure 12 and in elevation on figure 14.

• Welded to the sides of each rib are four sets of steel flanges leading to the glass fixings. The flanges are shown on plan in figure 13 and in elevation on figure 14. The glass fixings attached to ends of the steel flanges incorporate a central pin (formed of two screws inserted from opposite ends and meeting in the middle) that allows a measure of rotation within the fixing, thus enabling the glass sheets below to assume whatever angle is needed to form the canopy curve.

• The canopy is laterally stabilised by a forked link to the column at each side [figures 3 and 4] and by a set of perimeter tendons marked R, S, T and U on figure 2.

Conclusion

After four years the Bracken House canopy is still in excellent condition except that the clear silicone joints have yellowed and the lights have not been cleaned and replaced as necessary, leaving a few random spots of light instead of the delightful sparkle seen in figure 1. To avoid the first problem, the architects would now specify black rather than clear silicone. The second problem rests with the building owners: dare one hope that they may read these lines and wake up to their curatorial responsibilities for one of the finest buildings in the City of London?

SUMMARY DATA

Client:
Obayashi Europa BV
Architects:
Sir Michael Hopkins & Partners, London
Structural design:
Ove Arup & Partners, London
Quantity Surveyor:
Northcroft Neighbour and Nicholson, London
Main contractor:
Trollope & Colls Construction Limited, London
Glazing contractor:
MBM, Germany
Specification of tendons:
PVC bead blasted stainless steel solid rods of the following diameters [see figure 2]:
H I J K N - 38.0mm   T - 22.0mm

A B D F L - 33.7mm   E - 21.3mm
C G M O R - 27.0mm   U - 18.0mm
S - 25.0mm
Specification of ribs:
Brushed stainless steel hollow tubes with an outer diameter of 71mm and an inner diameter of 45mm.
Specification of glass:
19mm-thick laminated toughened clear glass, fritted.
Specification of joints:
Clear structural silicone sealant
Total cost of canopy:
£65,000
Life expectancy:
Canopy overall: indefinite; silicone joints: 25 years if regularly washed

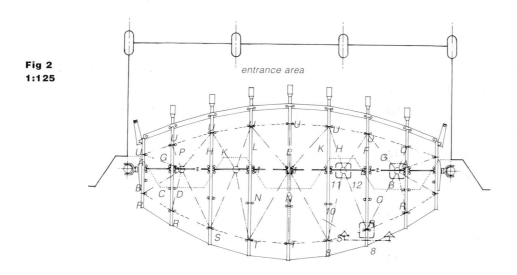

Fig 2
1:125

entrance area

Fig 3
1:125

lighting fittings

back edge of canopy
turned up to form gutter

RWP

rainwater hopper

lateral anchor

building facade over

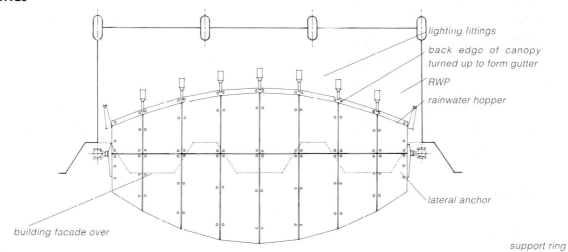

Fig 4
1:125

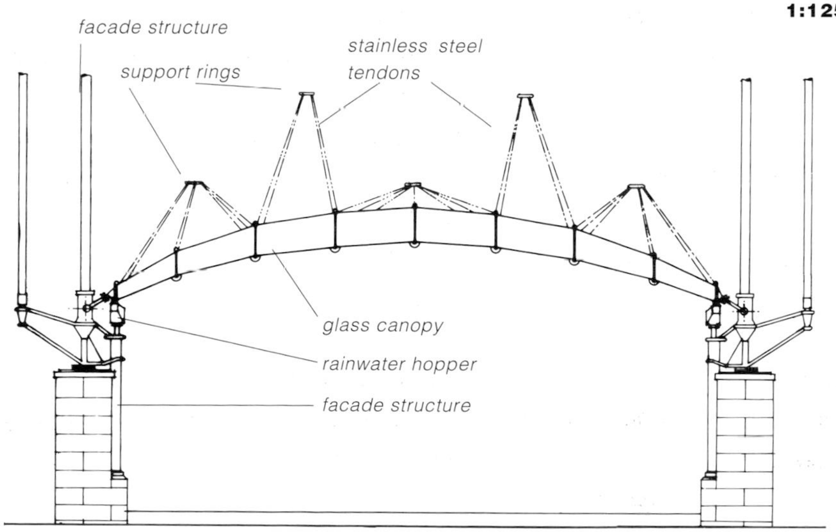

facade structure

support rings

stainless steel
tendons

glass canopy

rainwater hopper

facade structure

Fig 5
1:125

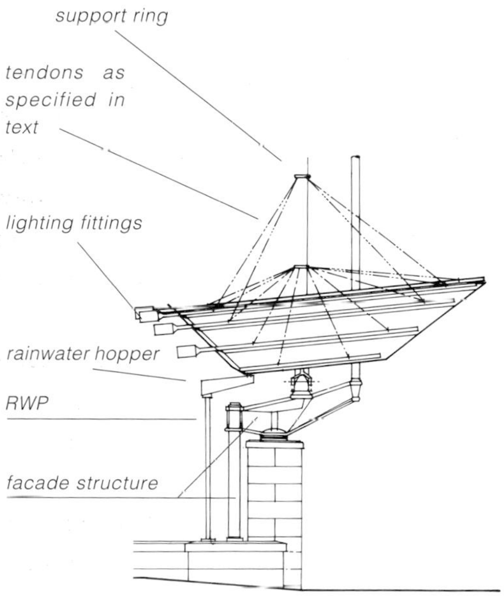

support ring

tendons as
specified in
text

lighting fittings

rainwater hopper

RWP

facade structure

2. Plan of canopy
from above; 3.
Reflected plan of
canopy under-
side; 4. Front
elevation; 5. Side
elevation

Fig 6   **Fig 7**   **Fig 8**

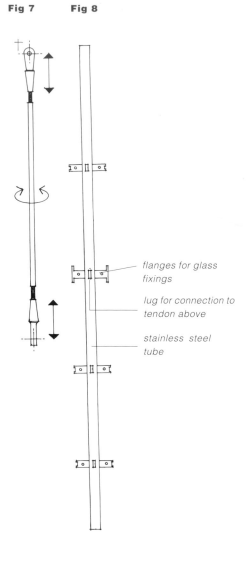

flanges for glass fixings

lug for connection to tendon above

stainless steel tube

Fig 9

6. Bracken House Entrance Canopy, London; 7. Typical stainless steel tendon; 8. Typical rib; 9. Canopy suspension detail

Fig 10
1:10

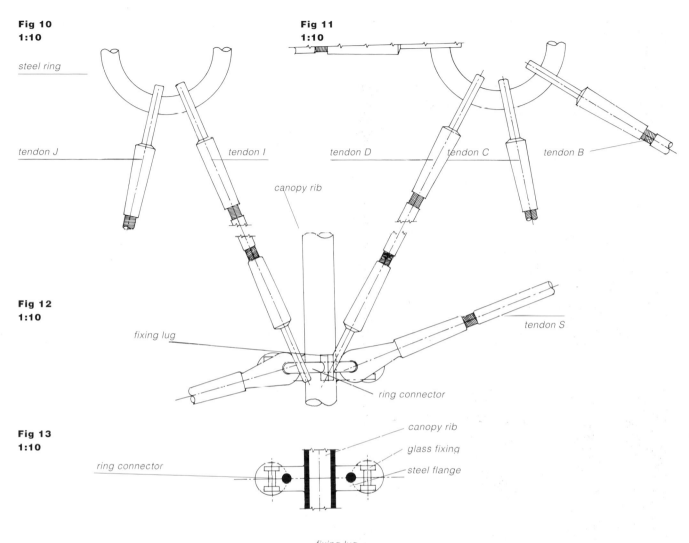

steel ring

tendon J   tendon I

Fig 11
1:10

tendon D   tendon C   tendon B

canopy rib

Fig 12
1:10

fixing lug

tendon S

ring connector

Fig 13
1:10

canopy rib

glass fixing

ring connector

steel flange

Fig 14

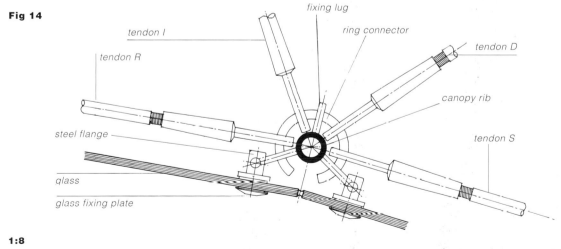

tendon I

tendon R

fixing lug

ring connector

tendon D

canopy rib

tendon S

steel flange

glass

glass fixing plate

1:8

10. Ring at high level; 11. Ring at lower level; 12. Detail of connection between tendons and canopy; 13. Plan of flanged connection detail; 14. Detail elevation of connection between tendons and canopy

Fig 1

RAFAEL VINOLY ARCHITECTS AND DEWHURST MACFARLANE & PARTNERS

YURAKUCHO SUBWAY CANOPY, TOKYO INTERNATIONAL FORUM

Tokyo

Tokyo's £1.5 billion International Forum is the largest architectural project to be realised in Tokyo this century, and a *tour de force* of steel and glass design. We describe here only the canopy over the subway entrance stair. A critique of the Forum as a whole was published in the *Architectural Review* of November 1996 (pp37-45).

Brief

The subway canopy was the last phase of the Forum to be tackled. A glass canopy was envisaged, and the design needed to cope with:

• Normal imposed stresses such as thermal stress, wind and snow loads and impact.

• Earthquakes: seismic disturbances create particular problems for designers because they generate forces that act on a structure from many directions, not just a few as with gravity loads or wind uplift.

• Typhoons: acting on the particular geometry of the Yurakucho subway canopy, these could produce wind pressures three times greater than the anticipated wind pressure for a similar structure in Britain or Europe.

• Remaining safe under the above conditions even after removal of 60 per cent of the structure.

Original Design Concept

The original proposal in July 1995 was for a 10 x 5 metre glass roof supported by three cantilevered steel beams. When a selected group of subcontractors gathered round the model in September to study the proposal, the Japanese project engineer suggested that the steel beam configuration was unnecessarily complex and that an all-glass structure would be preferable. The architects agreed and the main contractor asked the structural consultants to produce a structural glass design.

The architects decided almost at once to develop a cantilever structure based on toughened glass fins similar to those used for bracing curtain walls against wind pressure, but little progress was made on the new design. Finally, knowing of their reputation in innovative glass design, the Japanese structural consultant called Dewhurst Macfarlane & Partners to seek advice.

All-Glass Design Concept

The enlarged design team quickly agreed on the principle of a glass canopy supported on three glass cantilevered beams. However, there was a problem: Dewhurst Macfarlane's previous applications of this concept had never exceeded a span of six metres and could use

1. Yurakucho subway canopy, Tokyo International Forum, Tokyo

one unjointed length of glass to form the entire cantilever. The Tokyo proposal was for a cantilever of almost nine metres, requiring each cantilevered beam to be built up from separate lengths of glass glued to a plastic interleaf acting as a full-strength bonding layer.

This was risky in that all available plastic laminates suffer from creep deformation. This leads to excessive deflection, which may in turn lead to the collapse of a beam relying on such laminated construction to resist long-term stress. The risk was especially great in the Tokyo situation with its susceptibility to typhoons and earthquakes.

Back in London, Tim Macfarlane ruminated for a week before having an idea over dinner. In time-honoured fashion he sketched it on a paper napkin [figure 4] and that same evening, 29 October 1995, developed the sketch into a scale drawing and a set of calculations. The design incorporated what would later be known as the 'bezel connection'.

Detailed Design

The canopy top consists of two 19-millimetre glass sheets laminated together, supported by three glass/acrylic beams as shown in figure 8. Each of the three beams is built up from a sequence of five blade types and diminishes in cross section as it proceeds from the canopy base (where the bending moment is greatest) to its outer edge (where the bending moment is least). The cross sections at various points from base to outer edge are as follows:
• Figure 6A: at the base, an outer pair of 41-millimetre glass blades (formed of two 19-millimetre toughened glass sheets laminated together) enclose an inner pair of 40-millimetre single-thickness acrylic blades making four blades in total. The blades are interleaved with, and bolted through, a pair of Y-shaped steel blades anchoring the canopy to its foundation.
• Figure 6B: next, two outer pairs of laminated glass blades enclose three acrylic blades.
• Figure 6C: next, an outer pair of laminated glass blades enclose one acrylic blade.
• Figure 6D: next, there is a pair of laminated glass blades, with no further acrylic elements.
• Figure 6E: finally, approaching the outer edge of the canopy, there is one single laminated glass blade.

Each sandwich of blades is bolted together by 40-millimetre diameter high-strength stainless steel pins passing though 68-millimetre diameter holes in the glass, as shown in plan of figure 11 and in section in figure 9. Loads are distributed by the three-part metal bezels shown in black in figure 9.

To avoid the generation of dangerously high local stresses in the glass around each bezel by inaccurate fit, the chamfered profile of each hole in the glass was machined to extreme accuracy, thus ensuring full engagement between glass and steel interfaces and the development of maximum joint strength.

Fabrication

The five-metre long glass blades were cut to shape by a computer-controlled cutting machine by FA Firmans, and then ground and polished to precise dimensions and a smooth finish. The finished sheets were then tough-

Fig 2

Fig 3

Fig 4

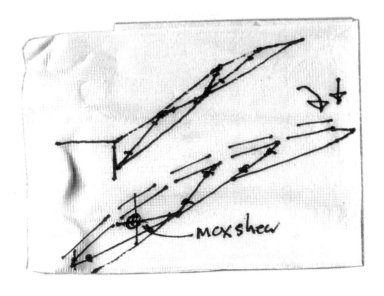

2. The canopy seen from behind; 3. Close-up of glass finish; 4. Tim Macfarlane's sketch on a paper napkin

ened, again at the Firmans workshop in East London. Like most such equipment the machine was designed only for sheets of up to 3.5 metres long, but with the ends of the machine taken off, sheets as long as seven metres can be toughened by feeding in first one end and then the other.

Finally the toughened glass blades were laminated in pairs.

Erection

While the holes in the glass to take the steel bezels were machined with extreme precision, the bolting together of the glass and steel components on site could not be assumed to be similarly accurate. To avoid all risk of looseness, each bezel was therefore drilled slightly off-centre, and fitted with an insert also drilled off-centre, and by rotation of the two elements an extremely close fit could be achieved.

Allowance for Structural Movement

As at Bracken House, the canopy is small enough not to need special provision for movement, the latter being adequately catered for by the compressibility/extendability of the two-part polysulphide structural sealant connecting the overhead panes.

Conclusion

The canopy was completed at the end of October 1996 and since then has endured two typhoons and a tremor registering six on the Richter scale, with no apparent problems.

SUMMARY DATA

Client:

Tokyo Metropolitan Government

Timetable:

Design commencement of all-glass concept: November 1995; design approved March 1996; construction completed October 1996

Architects:

Rafael Vinoly Architects

Structural design overall:

Structural Design Group

Structural design of glass canopy:

Dewhurst Macfarlane and Partners, London

Quantity Surveyor:

Futaba, Tokyo

Main contractor:

Taisei Contracting, Tokyo

Glass subcontractor:

Asahi Glass, Tokyo

Glass fabricator:

FA Firmans (Harold Wood Ltd), London

Glass and acrylic:

The glass fins are made of two 19mm toughened glass blades laminated together to form a 41mm sandwich. The acrylic fins consist of a single 40mm thickness of polymethalmethacrylate (pmma)

Total cost of canopy:

£1 million

Life expectancy:

Canopy overall: indefinite; Structural sealant: 25 years if regularly washed

5. Side view of canopy; 6. Detailed sections A to E through typical blade

Fig 5

Fig 6

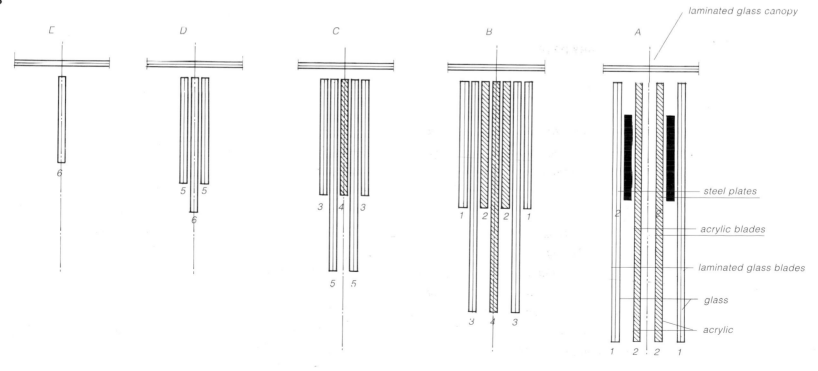

laminated glass canopy

E

D

C

B

A

6

5   5

6

3   4   3

5   5

3   4   3

1   2   2   1

1   2   2   1

2   2

1   2   2   1

steel plates

acrylic blades

laminated glass blades

glass

acrylic

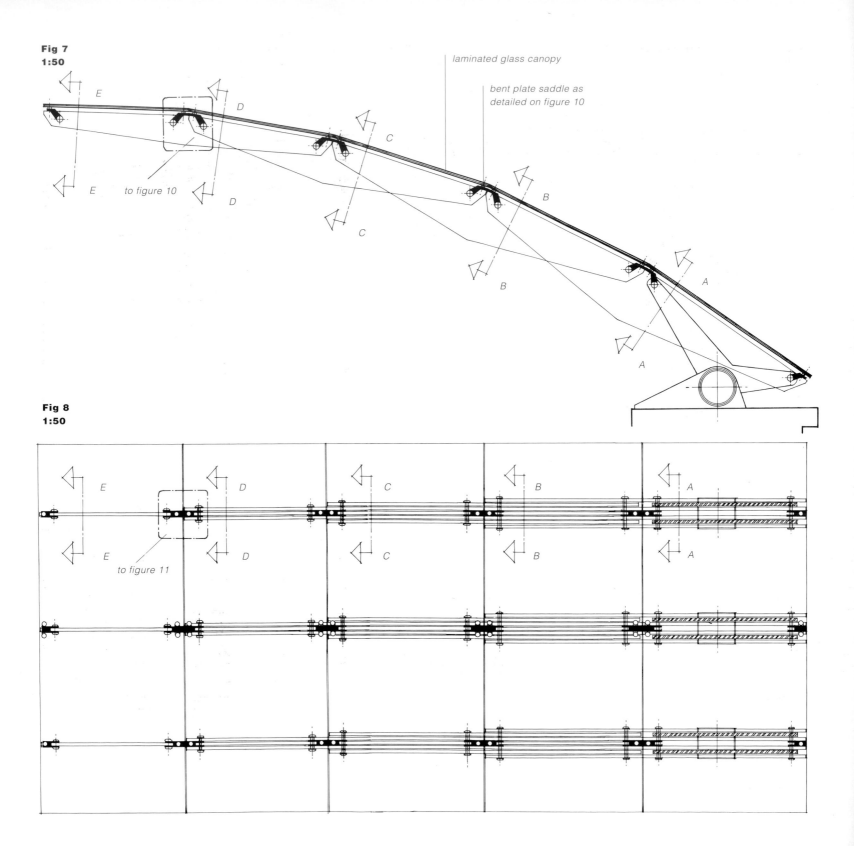

Fig 7
1:50

E

D

laminated glass canopy

bent plate saddle as
detailed on figure 10

C

E

to figure 10

D

C

B

B

A

A

Fig 8
1:50

E

D

C

B

A

E

to figure 11

D

C

B

A

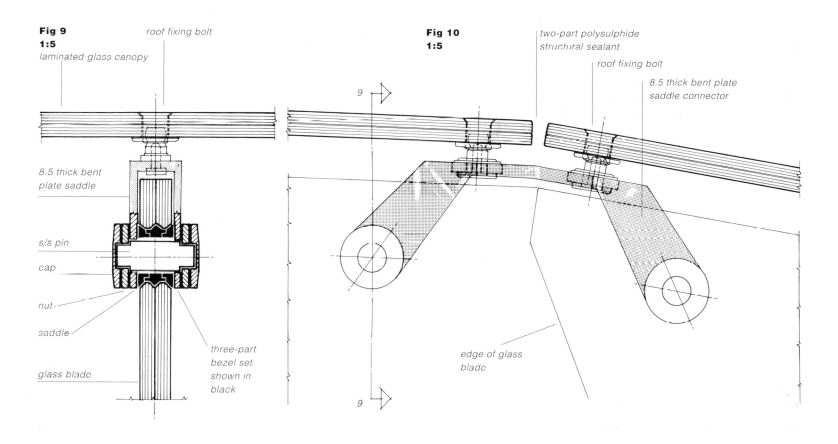

Fig 9
1:5

roof fixing bolt

laminated glass canopy

8.5 thick bent
plate saddle

s/s pin

cap

nut

saddle

glass blade

three-part
bezel set
shown in
black

Fig 10
1:5

9

9

two-part polysulphide
structural sealant

roof fixing bolt

8.5 thick bent plate
saddle connector

edge of glass
blade

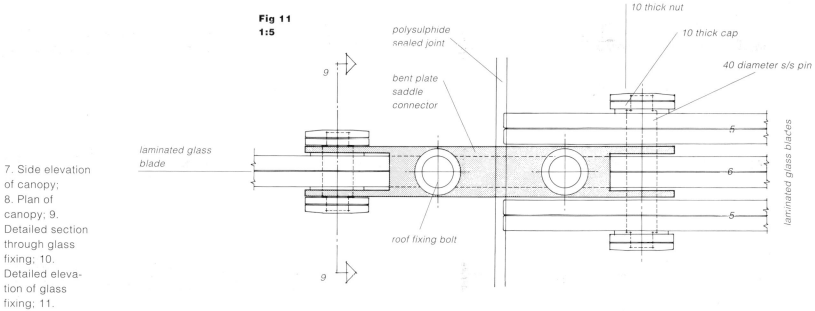

Fig 11
1:5

9

9

laminated glass
blade

polysulphide
sealed joint

bent plate
saddle
connector

roof fixing bolt

10 thick nut

10 thick cap

40 diameter s/s pin

5

6

5

laminated glass blades

7. Side elevation
of canopy;
8. Plan of
canopy; 9.
Detailed section
through glass
fixing; 10.
Detailed eleva-
tion of glass
fixing; 11.
Detailed plan of
glass fixing

FURTHER READING

History of Glass-roofed Building Types

1 Hix, John, *The Glass House*, Phaidon Press, London, 1996. A richly informative history of the development of the horticultural glass house. Beautifully produced with many full-colour illustrations.

2 Binney, Marcus and Pearce, David (eds), *Railway Architecture*, Orbis, London, 1979. Histories of the railway station mostly concentrate on the head building rather than the metal and glass shed behind. This reference probably gives the best (though still limited) coverage of the development of the shed.

3 Geist, Johann Friedrich, *Arcades: the History of a Building Type*, MIT Press, Cambridge Massachusetts, 1983. The standard history of galleria etc. Currently o/p.

The two most significant nineteenth century examples of glass-roofed exhibition halls are admirably described in the following volumes from Phaidon's *Architecture in Detail* series:

4 McKean, John, *Crystal Palace*, Phaidon Press, London, 1994.

5 Durant, Stuart and Low, Angus, *Palais des Machines*, Phaidon Press, London, 1994.

6 Saxon, Richard, *Atrium Buildings: Design and Development*, Architectural Press, London, 1986. Brief history, excellent technical coverage and gazetteer of notable examples in UK and USA. While outdated in minor regards (eg, fire safety legislation) this remains an excellent basic reference.

7 Saxon, Richard, *The Atrium Comes of Age*, Longman, Harlow, 1994. A natural supplement to (6) which it updates in all respects, most importantly in terms of fire safety.

Glass as a Material

8 Button, David and Pye, Brian, *Glass in Building*, Butterworth Architecture, Oxford, 1993. Comprehensive and authoritative guide to all technical aspects, produced with the technical support of Pilkington. Clearly written and attractively produced with many excellent full-colour illustrations.

9 Wigginton, Michael, *Glass in Architecture*, Phaidon Press, London, 1996. Covers partly the same ground as (8) but includes useful case studies of glass in architecture (most of the latter being glass walls, not roofs, but still perfectly relevant) and delves more deeply into the possibilities of future technical advances. Technically informative and lavishly produced with many full-colour illustrations.

10 Rice, Peter and Dutton, Hugh, *Structural Glass*, A & FN Spon, London, 1995. A welcome translation of the second edition of *Le Verre Structurel* published in 1995 by Editions du Moniteur, Paris. Co-written by the late, great Peter Rice, this essential reference contains thoughts on design philosophy, notes on technical design and thirteen case examples.

Overhead Glazing

11 BS 5516:1991 'Code of Practice for Vertical and Sloping Patent Glazing' is the only British regulation or standard giving any recommendations about the use of glass in roofs. Its provisions apply only to patent glazing, and cover only the more modest end of the range in terms of scale, but the advice on glass selection is broadly applicable to all non-agricultural roof glazing or canopies. Its key provisions are included in Table 2 on page 9.